Blood, Bread, and Fire

THE CHRISTIAN'S THREE-FOLD EXPERIENCE

By
VANCE HAVNER
PASTOR, FIRST BAPTIST CHURCH, CHARLESTON, S. C.
Author, "*Amos, the Prophet with a Modern Message*,"
"*By the Still Waters*," "*Consider Him*,"
"*Secret of Christian Joy*"

SECOND EDITION

ZONDERVAN PUBLISHING HOUSE
GRAND RAPIDS   MICHIGAN

COPYRIGHT, MCMXXXIX, BY
ZONDERVAN PUBLISHING HOUSE

EIGHT-FIFTEEN FRANKLIN STREET
GRAND RAPIDS, MICHIGAN

Printing Statement:

Due to the very old age and scarcity of this book, many of the pages may be hard to read due to the blurring of the original text, possible missing pages, missing text and other issues beyond our control.

Because this is such an important and rare work, we believe it is best to reproduce this book regardless of its original condition.

Thank you for your understanding.

PREFACE

In presenting a second set of sermons to our readers, we are endeavoring to gather up chiefly from several Christian magazines, a number of our messages which the Lord has blessed to His glory. In His Name we offer them with the prayer that they may fulfill in some measure the prophet's responsibility to speak to edification and exhortation and comfort (I Cor. 14:3).

We gratefully acknowledge permission granted by the following magazines for publication of most of the sermons contained herein:

To *Revelation*, Philadelphia, for "Three Perils of Christian Discipleship," "Playing in the Marketplace," "What is a Christian?" "Needed . . . a Prophet."

To *Moody Monthly*, Chicago, for "Shall We Crown or Crucify Jesus?" and "What is Your Life?"

To *Light*, Hollywood, Calif., for "Blood, Bread, and Fire."

To *King's Business*, Los Angeles, for "But God . . ."

V. H.

Charleston, S. C.

CONTENTS

I.	Blood, Bread, and Fire	9
II.	Shall We Crown or Crucify Jesus?	17
III.	Three Perils of Christian Discipleship	25
IV.	Playing in the Market-Place	35
V.	What Is a Christian?	45
VI.	Needed — a Prophet	55
VII.	"What Is Your Life?"	62
VIII.	"And He Stood Speechless"	70
IX.	"Entered Into Rest"	77
X.	Where Are You at Calvary?	86
XI.	"But God —"	97
XII.	"Faith in Christ Jesus"	105

I

BLOOD, BREAD, AND FIRE

THE Christian life is an experience of blood, bread, and fire.

Of all the accusations hurled at the gospel, none is more ridiculous than that it is pale and uninteresting. Of course, we do not expect the natural man to be charmed by it. Unto us who believe and unto us only, is Christ precious. But, contrary to popular notion, the most pale and insipid experience on earth is a life without Christ. The fact is, the unbeliever is dead, and a dead man certainly is not a very colorful spectacle. If sinners are dead in trespasses and sins, and if "she that liveth in pleasure is dead while she liveth," then every haunt of sin is a morgue and every frolic of the devil is a funeral.

Sometimes we listen to these poor, animated corpses all excited over their little tempests in teapots, chattering away in a "much ado about nothing," and we wonder how people can talk so much and say so little. The styles, the latest movies, the races, the baseball scores, the latest jokes (most of them a hundred years old)—one listens and hopes that presently they will strike something more serious. But no, they have struck bottom; this is their life. Then we think of the heroes of faith who marched through this earth moving mountains by the might of God, and we could laugh were it not so pitiable—these poor souls who say that being a Christian is such an uninteresting way to live!

But perhaps they got their idea from watching some professing Christians who are terribly poor advertisements of the faith. Certainly if the gospel could do no more for us than some professing Christians have allowed it to do for them, it would be a tame affair. We have sat in some churches through a dreary service, a lifeless round of uprisings and downsittings, and found it hard to think of that assembly following in the train of the early "fools for Christ's sake," who upset a world.

Yet we should not judge the faith by its worst representatives. There are many who have proved the Christian life to be what it really is—a mighty experience of blood, bread, and fire. When the average man thinks of a Christian, he thinks of churches and choirs, preachers and prayers, perhaps blue laws and Puritanic restrictions. Few think of a Christian as the greatest of miracles, a sinner saved through the blood of Christ, sustained by the bread of Christ, aflame with the heavenly fire.

The Christian life is, first of all, an experience of blood, for, however unpleasant it may be to some sensitive souls, the gospel is soaked and saturated with the crimson flood of Calvary. "Without shedding of blood there is no remission of sins." The sacrifices of Cain may please the aesthetic, but the gory lamb of Abel found favor with God. We may scribble lovely things on the door-posts, but it is the blood applied that wards off the avenging angel. It is not Christ the paragon, but Christ the propitiation, Who saves from sin. Critics may scorn a "bloody gospel" and "slaughter-house theology"; the blood songs may be taken from our hymnals, and professors may even teach that Jesus was tied to the cross instead of nailed there; but for all that, He still declares to the Greeks who would see Jesus, "And I, if I be lifted up from the earth, will draw all men unto me," and it is the shed blood of a Calvary Christ, not the idealism of a crystal Christ, that makes the sinner white as snow.

Our redemption is through His blood (Eph. 1:7). We are redeemed with His precious blood, not with silver and gold (I Pet. 1:18). He purchased the church with His blood (Acts 20:28). His blood is the ground of forgiveness, for it was shed for many for the remission of sins (Matt. 26:28). It is the ground of justification (Rom. 5:9) and our peace, since He made peace through the blood of His cross (Col. 1:20). By His blood we have access to God, for we who sometimes were far off are made nigh by the blood of Christ (Eph. 2:13) and we have boldness to enter into the holiest by the blood of Christ (Heb. 10:19). By His blood we have daily cleansing, for if we walk in the light as He is in the light . . . His blood cleanses from all sin (I John 1:7).

This, then, is the way of the cross and of course

it is foolishness to the natural man. If Christ had propounded a clever philosophy or preached a lavender-and-rosewater idealism, men would gladly be His disciples, but to live through One Who died and to be saved by One Who could not save Himself, and above all to be saved through the merits of His shed blood—nothing could be more repulsive to the wiseacres of earth. But whether the fastidious like it or not, there stands the word of our God: "When I see the blood, I will pass over you." When we come to God convicted of sin and repentant toward Him and receive by faith His Son into our hearts, then the provisions of the blood become effectually ours; we have reached the first phase of the Christian life, the experience of blood.

But the blood must be followed by the bread. After the Passover blood was applied, the Passover Lamb was eaten. Christ is not only the Passover Lamb, Whose blood saves, but also the Passover feast, the bread of life. The Christian life begins with Christ, the slain Lamb of God, and the blood applied. But it continues on the strength of Christ, the Passover feast, as we feed upon Him by faith. The blood must be followed by the bread, for except we eat His flesh and drink His blood, we have no life in us (John 6: 53). The Lord's Supper sets forth, among other things, the bread of life, Christ our sustenance as well as Christ our Savior.

The Jews in Egypt ate all of the lamb; Christ in His fulness must be appropriated by faith for every need. They ate it then, not later; and the time to feed upon Christ is now. They ate it with bitter herbs; and Christ must be received with a humble and contrite heart. They ate it ready to travel: the Christian is a pilgrim and stranger and must feed upon Christ as one whose citizenship is in heaven and who is seeking a city and bound for another country. There was no work connected with the Passover; nor must the believer mix his own works with the finished work of grace. The lamb was eaten with unleavened bread; and so must we purge our hearts of the leaven of sin and wickedness if we are to feed upon Christ. How unworthily do men partake of the Lord's Supper, which symbolizes our feeding upon Christ! Verily, they drink judgment to themselves and are guilty of the body and blood of the Lord. No wonder many are weak and sickly and many sleep!

But how do we feed upon the bread of life? Our Lord made it clear once for all when He said to those who were puzzled at His teaching: "It is the spirit that quickeneth; the flesh profiteth nothing: the *words* that I speak unto you, they are spirit, and they are life" (John 6: 63). To feed upon Him is to read and to heed His words, to hear and keep His commandments. If we abide in Him and His *words* abide in us, we shall ask what we will and it shall be done unto us (John 15:7). If we love Him we will keep His *words*, and the Father will love us, and the Father and Son will come to us and abide with us (John 14:23). Heaven and earth shall pass away, but His *words* shall never pass away (Mark 13: 31). But whosoever shall be ashamed of Him and His *words* in this adulterous and sinful generation, of him also shall the Son of man be ashamed, when He comes in the glory of His Father with the holy angels (Mark 8: 38).

Christ, the bread, may seem hard doctrine. It seemed so when He Himself preached it and some asked, "Who can hear it?" He may have to ask some of us, as He asked long ago, "Will ye also go away?" God grant that we may answer as did Peter, "Lord, to whom shall we go? Thou hast the *words* of eternal life. And we believe and are sure that thou art that Christ, the Son of the living God" (John 6: 68-69).

To feed upon the bread, then, is to read the Word of God, to pray over it, to meditate upon it, and then go out to observe and do it. Many Christians who know the safety of the blood do not correspondingly know as they ought the strength of the bread. The blood makes safe: the bread makes strong. The Christian begins his life by coming under the blood for salvation; but he continues by the blood for daily cleansing and the bread for daily food.

But still the Christian life is not complete: there must be the experience of fire, the fire of Pentecost, the fire of the Holy Spirit for power in service and testimony. The early Christians in the upper room had come under the blood; they had fed upon the Word of Christ, the bread, some of them for three years. Yet He bade them tarry until they were fire-baptized. The blood makes safe and the bread makes strong but more is needed for witnessing. And it is just here that thousands of believers fall short with a pre-Pentecost experience. They have been taught that a personal knowledge of Christ is all that one needs, which is true as to salvation, but it is overlooked that these Christians knew the Lord yet they must wait for power.

It is true that Pentecost, historically, took place once for all. So did Calvary. But each individual must personally appropriate the blood by faith and so must each believer receive by faith the Spirit for power. The promise of the Spirit is received by faith (Gal. 3: 14). It is an experience of spiritual thirst, then coming to Christ, drinking of the Spirit by faith, believing and overflowing (John 7: 37-39).

So the blood and bread must be accompanied by fire. We have fundamentalism and facts; we have activity and earnestness and sincerity; we even have blood-washed and blood-nourished Christians, well-taught in the Word, who still lack fire. Some are prejudiced against it, identifying any definite experience of the Spirit with fanaticism. Some see nothing but a gradual growth in grace. Some mistake the indwelling of the Spirit for the infilling. Some have "received" with a cheap and easy "believism" who somehow did not receive after all. For many reasons the church is largely behind closed doors as before Pentecost, and believers try to stir up a fire from their own sparks instead of being set on fire of God.

We are not here advocating some wild and weird emotional experience, but we do hold that he who seeks to burn out for God will have to go deeper than sentence prayers and occasional wishful thinking. There must be a holy heartburn and a consuming longing for the fulness of the Spirit. Tears and fastings and all night prayers have no value of themselves, but God will reward the man who forgets all else seeking the double portion of "power with God and men." It is not that God is stingy and must be coaxed, for He "giveth liberally and upbraideth not." It is that we ourselves are so shallow and sinful that we need to tarry before Him until our restless natures can be stilled and the clamor of outside voices be deadened so that we can hear His voice. Such a state is not easily reached, and the men God uses have paid a price in wrestlings and prevailing prayer. But it is such men who rise from their knees confident of His power and go forth to speak with authority and not as the scribes.

> *I saw a human life ablaze with God;*
> *I felt a power divine*
> *As through an empty vessel of frail clay*
> *I saw God's glory shine.*
> *Then woke I from a dream, and cried aloud:*
> *"My Father, give to me*
> *The blessing of a life consumed by God,*
> *That I may live for Thee!"*

The blood, the bread, the fire—may yours be the trinity of a full experience!

II

SHALL WE CROWN OR CRUCIFY JESUS?

What then shall I do with Jesus which is called Christ?
—MATT. 27: 22

WE live in a strange world. Scientifically it is round; spiritually it is flat, and it never has been more flat than it is now. It has become the fashion of the times to sneer at all venerable institutions. We live in a calloused generation that ridicules all the sanctities of life. And it is not surprising that the Christian faith should be attacked by these literary snipers with whom a little learning has become indeed a dangerous thing.

The old-time religion, by which we mean the historical faith of our fathers and not the hysterical faith of some today, is being assaulted by hordes of fools who rush in where angels fear to tread. But we Bible Christians feel no alarm. Like Paul from the Philippian dungeon, we would say to these assailants, "Do thyself no harm, for we are all here." We are not losing sleep for fear that some scientist will dig the foundations of our faith from under us nor are we worried over the critic's vials of scorn. The obsequies have been pronounced before now over a supposedly dead Christianity, but the "corpse" has always come to life in the midst of the interment to outlive all the pallbearers.

We do not expect to make a "hit" with the times. We are not surprised to be rated in some minds along with the family carry-all as relics of a simple-minded past, to be greeted in some quarters like poor relations come to town. After all, this generation is not so "smart." About the really great matters of life it knows less than any generation before it. It simply uses longer words to tell what it does not know. We lead the world in mass production, but we have failed in man production. We produce, but we do not create. Other generations left art galleries; we leave signboards. We have printing-presses, but no Shakespeares; radios, but no Demosthenes; pulpits, but no Pauls. We can turn out fiddles by the thousands, but no one can make a Stradivarius. We print books by the millions, but who is writing anything worthy of such distribution? We sends words around the world in split seconds, but who is saying anything worth sending around the world? Never has a generation traveled so fast and covered so little ground. Modern youth, forgetting that it is training for a race, lives as though racing for a train.

There are those who imagine that nobody really believes the Bible any more except intellectual throwbacks in rural Podunks, back-number preachers with "Mother Goose" mentalities. But there are still thousands who have not bowed the knee to Baal and not all of them are down in the "Boll Weevil Belt" either! Our views are not fashionable, but our faith has proved its case long ago, and any generation that has made as big a clown of itself as this one has no business criticizing the faith of its fathers.

Certainly the foundations of this country were laid in the light of this faith. We Bible Christians are not the ones who today honeycomb the land with class hatred. It is not we who are destroying the sanctity of human life, home, and marriage. It is not we who are undermining the institutions of law and order. It is not we who are corrupting a true patriotism with a false pacifism. If we are derided for still preaching the old Bible, we submit that we prefer a text from Moses to a theme from Moscow!

We insist that the supreme issue before men today is the old, old question, "Shall we crown or crucify Jesus?" Those who have seen the original of Munkacsy's painting, "Christ before Pilate," will remember how the artist makes the figure of the Lord Jesus stand out from all the rest. He is still on trial in the midst of this age, and among all other issues He stands supreme. On that historic occasion, Pilate faced the greatest question of all time, "What shall I do then with Jesus which is called Christ?" A lot of water has run under the bridge since then, but still the supreme issue with individuals and nations is, "What about Jesus Christ?"

In this trial of the ages, Pilate faced three alternatives. First, he asked Jesus, "Art thou a king?" Jesus declared that His kingdom is a kingdom of truth, and that everyone who is of the truth hears His voice. I imagine that Pilate must have shrugged his shoulders as he asked wearily, "What is truth?" He had listened to Oriental jugglers and Roman lawyers and Greek philosophers ranting about truth until he was in no position to believe that standing before him was One Who not only knows the truth but is the Truth. So, standing before the greatest alternative of his life, he did what millions have done since, he crowned the cynic and crucified Christ.

The first alternative therefore was

CYNICISM OR CHRIST

We live in the age of the cynic who sees the price of everything and the value of nothing. It is a strange day when the less one is sure of, the more he is supposed to know. If a minister says, "We may well suppose," he is counted brilliant. If he declares, "Thus saith the Lord," he is called a fanatic and a bigot. This generation calls itself "hard-boiled," but really it is just "half-baked," like Ephraim, who was "a cake not turned."

Nobody need ask today, "What is truth?" for the truth has been revealed. The Lord Jesus Christ said, "I am the truth," and if any man will do His will he shall know of the doctrine. Coleridge said the test of Christianity is, "Try it." "The proof of the pudding is the eating." Anyone can know the truth if he will take Christ at His word and see what happens. We shall turn question-marks of uncertainty into exclamation-points of conviction if we quit asking, "What is truth?" and learn that truth is not a "what" but a "whom," and rest our souls on a Person, not upon a philosophy.

Our Lord said, "Ye shall know the truth, and the truth shall make you free" (John 8: 32). The secret of freedom is to know the truth, and the secret of truth is to know the Son. "If the Son therefore shall make you free, ye shall be free indeed" (John 8: 36). The natural man cannot know the truth any more than a blind man can appreciate a landscape, for the natural man receiveth not the things of the Spirit of God. "The heart has its reasons of which the reason knows nothing." Truth is learned by believing, then seeing. The intellectual doubter is really only a moral coward who is not willing to give the gospel a fair trial.

No one should criticize the gospel until he has tried it; then he will not criticize it. There are no reasons for being a cynic. There are excuses, but an excuse is only the skin of a reason stuffed with a lie. The Lord Jesus Christ made a fair proposition. He said that willingness to obey God's will would prove the claims of Christ.

Those who criticize the gospel are not honest enough to try it on its own terms. They are too ignorant to speak wisely about it, but not too wise to speak ignorantly. Let Christ prove Himself; He is His own defense. Come to Him as a sinner on His terms, not yours. After all, we are not sinners because we are skeptics; we are skeptics because we are sinners. Skepticism is only a smokescreen thrown before a sinful heart. Instead of cynically asking, "What is truth?" come to Him just as you are without one plea but that His blood was shed for you, and He will prove Himself to be the

"whom" where all your "whats" will find their answer.
The second alternative that Pilate faced was

Criminality of Christ

It was customary to release a prisoner at the Passover. He chose to release Barabbas and to crucify Christ. If we do not choose Christ, we choose the criminal. Life is a choice between the best or the beast, and when we crucify Christ, we release Barabbas.

It is very evident that Barabbas is loose in these tragic days. We lead the world in crime here in America, crime that has increased 1200 per cent in the last thirty-five years. Our annual murder rate is eleven to twelve thousand, and that is partly because murderers know that the chances are three to one that they will never be caught; twelve to one that if caught they will never be convicted; and a hundred to one that if caught and convicted they will never die for the crime.

Murder, robbery, kidnaping, immorality, suicide—these crowd the headlines in a day supposed to set the high-water mark for civilization. Jails and penitentiaries are filled with criminals under twenty-five. Our Pilgrim forefathers carried guns to church; we may soon find it necessary again to do the same. Criminality is the natural consequence of the rejection of the Lord Jesus Christ. When He is crucified in the souls and societies of men, Barabbas is set free. Christ is the only cure for crime. "If any man be in Christ, he is a new creature: old things are passed away; behold, all things are become new" (II Cor. 5: 17).

Pilate's third alternative was

CAESAR OR CHRIST

That was the finishing blow. Pilate sought to release Jesus, but the Jews cried, "If thou let this man go, thou art not Caesar's friend: whosoever maketh himself a king speaketh against Caesar" (John 19: 12). It was Caesar or Christ, and Pilate chose Caesar. Today that Rome has passed, and Caesar has passed, but Christ remains "the same yesterday, and today, and forever."

If we are strictly honest today, we must confess that most of us have no king but Caesar. We have sold out to the god of this age. Modern America is repeating the story of decadent Rome. We have gone wild over the same things. They wore purple robes and we wear dress suits, but the lust of the flesh, the lust of the eyes, and the pride of life are still our gods. We are a befuddled generation, sick of old conditions and unable to create better; too ignorant to explain life, too shallow to endure it, too bitter to enjoy it, too weak to overcome it. We are not transformed but conformed to this world, slaves of its fashions, disciples of its philosophies, devotees of its pleasures. Wrapped in ourselves, we make small packages. Our eyes are glued to stocks and bonds, clothes and cars, and all the tinsel trappings of life's mad masquerade.

Even in our church circles, we claim allegiance to Christ, but too often our tribute is to Caesar. Since Constantine embraced Christianity and made it fashionable, Christ has been betrayed in the house of His friends. We call Him "Lord, Lord," but we do not His commands. We sing and talk about Him, but under the auspices of His cause we live in Rome and do as Rome does.

Today we face the same alternatives that confronted Pontius Pilate. Shall we crown the cynic and try to find our way through the wilderness of life by the feeble candle of reason? Shall we take the way of the criminal, the way of the beast, instead of the best? Shall we crown Caesar and crucify the Christ?

Shall we crown or crucify Jesus? He is the answer to cynicism, because He is the truth. He is the answer to criminality, because when we put on the Lord Jesus Christ we do not fulfill the lusts of the flesh. He is the answer to Caesar, because in Him we become citizens of heaven. Let us crown Him now in our hearts that one day we may have part in the final coronation, when the nations will lay their tributes at His feet and crown Him Lord of all!

III

THREE PERILS OF CHRISTIAN DISCIPLESHIP

IN the last six verses of the ninth chapter of Luke, we have what might be called three gospel snapshots. Three incidents are related with two verses given to each incident. Three men suddenly appear, and then just as suddenly, they are gone. We never hear of them again, and the tantalizing brevity of it all leaves us wondering what became of them. But if they do not stay long before us, they stay long enough to illustrate three perils of Christian discipleship: the Peril of the Uncounted Cost, the Peril of the Unburied Corpse, and the Peril of the Unforsaken Circle.

It will be remembered that here we are dealing with discipleship, not salvation. There is a pleasant teaching going the rounds to the effect that all we need to do to be Christians is to catch the spirit of Jesus and come under the sway of His personality. But the natural man cannot follow Christ, and they that are in the flesh cannot please God. One might as well try to catch sunbeams with fishhooks as to try to lay hold of Christ with the faculties of unregenerated Adam.

We must be born again by the Holy Spirit through faith in the Lord Jesus Christ as our sin-bearer and Savior. Then, having become sons of God through faith in the Son of God, we are next challenged to deny self, take up the cross, and follow our Lord. It is, therefore, to twice-born believers who have set out to follow in His steps that we present three perils of Christian discipleship.

Consider, first, the Peril of the Uncounted Cost, as set forth in verses 57 and 58 of Luke 9: "And it came to pass, that, as they went in the way, a certain man said to him, Lord, I will follow thee whithersoever thou goest. And Jesus said unto him, Foxes have holes, and birds of the air have nests; but the Son of man hath not where to lay his head."

In the parallel account of Matthew, we read that this man was "a certain scribe" (Matt. 8: 19) and that throws much light on this matter. Up until this time most of our Lord's disciples had been fishermen, humble folk of lowly occupation. If He had had an eye to earthly advantage, He would have lost no time enlisting a scribe among His followers. Would it not add prestige to number a theologian among them? Would it not add influence to have at least one D.D. among the disciples? But with His usual perception, our Lord saw the tragic weakness in this man and answered him with the reminder that while foxes and birds had staying places, the Savior Himself had nowhere to lay His head. It was only another way of saying: "You only think you want to follow Me. Do you realize what you are undertaking? Have you counted the cost?" All through the Bible we have these quick-on-the-trigger enthusiasts who are fine self-starters but who bog up miserably on the middle mile. There was the mixed multitude that started out of Egypt with Moses, attracted by the display of God's power and the glamor of adventure. It looked very romantic and exciting, but out in the wilderness they went to pieces, a perfect type of that superficial crowd that will ride any bandwagon that passes by.

We have in our churches plenty of professors who make good soldiers in a dress-parade when the flags are waving and the bugles are blowing but who, having never counted the cost, are offended when persecution arises and the battle waxes dangerous. Of this sort were the Reubenites of Judges 5: 15-16, who had fine impulses and patriotic sentiments but stayed at home from the battle, at home in the quiet security of the sheepfolds. We have those in our churches who have plenty of sentiment but make no sacrifice; who sing lustily in the choir on Sunday but live lustfully in the world all week; the kind of people who, when a piano is to be moved, escape by carrying the bench! Such enthusiasts file down the aisles promising to follow Christ whithersoever He goes, but who, not having counted the cost, begin to build and are not able to finish.

Our Lord had to contend with these superficial disciples throughout His ministry. In John 2: 23-25 we read that many believed on His name when they saw the miracles He did, "But Jesus did not commit himself unto them, because he knew all men, and needed not that any should testify of man: for he knew what was in man." Notice that they *believed* when they *saw*. That is not God's way — *believing, then seeing,* so of course, the Lord could not endorse it. Our Lord had absolutely no confidence in human nature. We have been hearing a great deal lately about Christ's going around seeing the latent good in people and calling out their best qualities. But Jesus Christ had no confidence in man; He had confidence only in what God can do for man.

Most of our commencement addresses are variations of the old "Go out and express yourself" idea. As a schoolboy I used to listen to inspiring and perspiring orators tell me that I had within me a hidden giant, an Atlas or a Hercules, who only needed to be released, latent possibilities that only needed to be set free. I discovered that there was a giant within me truly enough, but he was the devil, and he was already free! But I thank God that I also learned that there is a stronger Man who can bind the strong man so that I can say, "He that is in me is greater than he that is in the world."

Our Lord had no confidence in superficial disciples who did not count the cost. Crowds did not deceive Him. We measure a minister by the size of his crowd, but in the sixth chapter of John the Lord Jesus preached a crowd away! They could not bear His sermon on the bread of life and fell away until only the irreducible minimum of faithful disciples remained, and even they were puzzled. Again in Luke 14: 25-33, another multitude followed Him, but He knew they did not mean business, so He turned upon them with that terrific challenge to forsake everything, and with the two illustrations of not counting the cost: the foolish builder, and the king going to war. Sifting church-members through that sifter, one finds plenty of chaff today!

We have made discipleship too easy. We live in an age that wants something for nothing. Duty and discipline are out of date. We have forgotten that we are to endure hardness, that Ananias told Paul what things he must suffer, not what a fine salary lay ahead. Salvation has become a nightcap instead of a helmet. Ours is an air-conditioned, upholstered, streamlined faith. We go to heaven in Pullmans and stop over at Vanity Fair for the week-ends. Instead of fleeing the City of Destruction, we are out to clean it up with a social gospel. Tunnels have been put through the Hill of Difficulty, and the dirt has been used to fill up the valley of Humiliation.

It is said that at the early church convention of Nice, of the three hundred and eighteen delegates there were not more than a dozen who did not bear upon their bodies the marks of suffering in Christ's name. A great deal of water has run under the bridge since those days. Cushions have supplanted crosses. Comfortable Christians sing, "Where He leads me, I will follow," but not having counted the cost, they begin what they are unable to finish. But we thank God that when we start in His strength, He who has begun a good work in us will perform it.

Consider, in the second place, the Peril of the Unburied Corpse: "And he said unto another, Follow me. But he said, Lord, suffer me first to go and bury my father. Jesus said unto him, Let the dead bury the dead: but go thou and preach the kingdom of God" (Luke 9:59-60).

The first man was too eager; this man is not eager enough. The Lord Himself calls this man and adds a command to preach the gospel. Now this man wanted to bury his father; why then did he receive such a stern reply? The trouble lies deep: he was the kind who was ready to follow after all the "ifs" and reservations and provisos had been attended to. There is also a word in his request that tells the tale: "Suffer me *first* to go and bury my father." Something else was ahead of Jesus, something more important than the kingdom.

In such case there is always something dead in the life that needs burying; there is a corpse somewhere but we are not to return for the funeral. Sometimes there are past memories. Some disciples never get anywhere because of living in the past, by the casket of the dead, in the graveyard of yesterday. God said to Joshua, "Moses my servant is dead: now therefore, arise!" They had wept for thirty days over Moses, and that is long enough to weep over anybody. Life is too short to spend sitting up with the dead.

Maybe there is a friendship, a fellowship of this world that needs to be forsaken. If a man hate not the dearest one for Christ's sake, he cannot be a disciple. Many a young Christian gets nowhere in discipleship because of being in love with an unsaved sweetheart. "She that liveth in pleasure is dead while she liveth" (I Tim. 5:6) and the young man who courts a gay worldling had better remember that God calls her a corpse, however animated she may appear!

And how we preachers need afresh to hear our Lord's stern words: "Let the dead bury their dead: but go thou and preach the kingdom of God!" We are forever running to this supper and that banquet, this committee-meeting and that convocation, pronouncing the invocation over this and the benediction over that, blessing a tombstone here and extolling a corpse yonder, just helping the dead bury their dead!

Whatever one's private interpretation of this verse, whether we hold that the Lord meant "Better the dead should be unburied," or "Let the dead in trespasses and sins bury the dead in trespasses and sins," our Lord certainly is saying: "You must give up the dead loves of earth. I will have no divided allegiances, no fondling of the carcasses of this world." We Christians must forsake the funeral parlors of this world, the corpses of old affections, if we are to follow Him Who is the resurrection and the life. There will always be plenty to assist in the funerals of earth without our help. His word to us is: "What is that to thee: follow thou me!"

Consider, finally, the Peril of the Unforsaken Circle: "And another also said, Lord, I will follow thee; but let me first go bid them farewell, which are at home at my house. And Jesus said unto him, No man, having put his hand to the plough, and looking back, is fit for the kingdom of God" (Luke 9:61-62). This man went a step beyond the last man: he said, "I will follow thee." But he added a tragic word, and we have here one of the saddest texts in the Bible: "Lord, I will follow thee—*but* . . . ."

At first thought, one would say, "Surely there is no danger here. This man wants only to bid his people good-by." But again there is a tell-tale phrase: "Them which are at home at my house." I know that sort— sedate, satisfied, smug, and settled, content to live in this world. I can hear them say to this man, "Now, don't get excited over this new preacher. This enthusiasm will soon blow over." And thus they would tone him down to the dreary lukewarmness of those who have never seen the heavenly vision. So our Lord abruptly heads off trouble with that stern pronouncement about putting one's hand to the plough and looking back.

It is as though He said, "If you are going with Me, let us go; if you are staying at home, stay; but My kingdom is no place for a man with his head turned one way and his feet the other. I will have no Lot's wives, no looking back to Egypt's fleshpots. You must forget the things that are behind."

We think here of Abraham's servant who went to look for a wife for Isaac. A man looking for a wife for himself needs all the guidance he can get; this man was looking for a wife for another and needed more guidance still! But God led him, and he found the girl, and then, just as he was ready to start home, an insidious temptation crept in. The girl's brother and mother said, "Let the damsel abide with us a few days, at the least ten; after that she shall go." It looked innocent enough to tarry awhile. Why hurry home? But the old servant was not caught off guard. He knew that a great many things could happen in ten days: the girl might get sick, the parents might change their minds, anything could happen. So he answered, "Hinder me not, seeing the Lord hath prospered my way; send me away that I may go to my master."

How the Christian pilgrim today needs to learn that ready answer when Satan would delay him and have him tarry there with what appears a most innocent excuse! If we have set out to follow the Lord, there is no time to linger even for farewells. Let not the devil detain you when God has prospered your way!

The worst enemies of the Christian are not among the infidels and atheists, but in that sedate circle that lives at home in this world, to whom a man is a crank if he takes the gospel seriously. I know who discouraged me most when I entered the ministry: it was that frigid circle who could shrug a shoulder and lift an eyebrow and say, "Be not righteous overmuch," in a fashion that, but for God's grace, would take the fire out of any man. They were not opposed to Christ; they were church people; but their sort has quenched the spirit in more Christians than have all the infidels. One can feel the spiritual temperature drop to zero in their presence. They have caused more crooked furrows than all the higher critics. When Christ calls us, we are not even to tell that crowd good-by. We are not to give the unburied corpses a funeral nor the unholy circle a farewell. We are not even to favor them with a parting glance, for the glance will become a look, the look will become a gaze, and the plough will be left in the furrow.

There is no place in Christian discipleship for divided allegiance. If we are not with our Lord, we are against Him, and if we gather not with Him, we scatter abroad. Let us fix our eyes upon Him and beware of the three perils as common now as long ago: the peril of the Uncounted Cost, the peril of the Unburied Corpse, and the peril of the Unforsaken Circle.

IV

PLAYING IN THE MARKET-PLACE

But whereunto shall I liken this generation? It is like unto children sitting in the markets, and calling unto their fellows, and saying, We have piped unto you and ye have not danced; we have mourned unto you, and ye have not lamented.—MATT. 11: 16-17

As the context shows, our Lord had in mind His own childish generation, and the Pharisees in particular. John the Baptist had come, wild, austere, ascetic, a stern and awful prophet of the wilderness, thundering divine judgments and calling to repentance. They did not like him. Then the Lord Jesus had come, sociable, friendly, easy to approach, eating with publicans and sinners. They did not like Him either. They called John a demoniac and Jesus a glutton. They were like spoiled children.

We still have such children in the market-places, plenty of them in the churches. They have been petted and pampered until no kind of preaching suits them. If the wrath of God is proclaimed, the preacher is too severe; if love is preached, the minister is too sentimental. Thousands of church people would go home highly offended were either John the Baptist or Jesus the Christ to occupy the pulpit next Sunday. We have encountered these children of the market-place many times in our ministry. If we spoke in a low tone we were dull; if we spoke in a loud tone, we were deafening. If we stood still they pronounced us statues; if we stirred about, we were labeled sensationalists. We were much distressed until we learned to identify and classify these babes of the market-place.

But I am particularly concerned with the fact that our Lord speaks of His generation as children *playing* in the markets. First they piped; they played wedding. Then they mourned; they played funeral. First they rejoiced, and then they wept. It looked real enough, but it was only make-believe. They did not mean it; they were only children playing in the market-place.

The human race in general today is only playing at life. A hurried, feverish generation gulps down its breakfast, bolts to the office and shop, races home through crazy traffic, reads the comic sheets, tunes in on a radio comedian, takes an aspirin tablet, and calls it a day. A superficial multitude of sheep without a shepherd, dabbling in a thousand things, tries to talk learnedly on many matters but only exposes a pitiful ignorance of all. Compare the poetry of today with the bards of old, modern music with the old masters, modern politicians who only run for things with the old statesmen who stood for things, and you behold a nation of manikins, dummies, a Punch-and-Judy show. For we are only children playing in the market-place,

PLAYING IN THE MARKET-PLACE

just pretending to live, acting parts in a silly comedy that turns out to be a tragedy, just trying to pose our way through a dramatized version of ourselves.

But we turn to the professing church to discover, alas, even as our Lord found it among the Pharisees, multitudes of children just playing at religion. First, they are children: not childlike as our Lord would have us be (Matt. 18:3) but childish. There are babes who ought to be grown, milk-feeders who should long ago have reached a meat-diet, still carnal and proclaiming it as the Scriptures reveal by envying and strife and divisions, walking as men, saying, "I am of Paul," and "I am of Apollos" (I Cor. 3:3-4). Christians who ought to be teachers must themselves be taught first principles and "are become such as have need of milk, and not of strong meat. For every one that useth milk is unskilful in the word of righteousness: for he is a babe. But strong meat belongeth to them that are of full age, even those who by reason of use have their senses exercised to discern both good and evil" (Heb. 5: 12-14). Newborn Christians are indeed to desire the sincere milk of the Word that they may grow thereby (I Pet. 2:2) and must be nurtured with greatest patience. But the problem of many a pastor and church is these children who will not grow up, spoiled, pouting, selfish, grumbling, overgrown babies of the market-place who will not be moved by any preacher, to whom even John the Baptist would be a demoniac and the Lord a glutton.

Then they were children *in the market-place.* Many childish Christians play at religion because they live in the market-place; they are at home in this world. They live to buy and sell, to get and to gain, their minds are taken up with profit and loss, laying up treasure on earth and not in heaven. Where their treasure is their heart is also, and the cares of this world and the deceitfulness of riches choke the Word, and they become unfruitful. As it was in the days of Noah and of Lot, so it is today; millions who name the name of Christ are more at home in the market-place than at the house of God, more satisfied in the shop than in the sanctuary. No wonder they only play at religion; no wonder their piety is but a hollow mockery; no wonder with their mouth they show much love but their heart goeth after their covetousness! "They say they are rich and increased with goods and have need of nothing and know not that they are wretched and miserable and poor and blind and naked."

But in Jesus' day, the market-place was not only a place of buying and selling: it was the public square where the people met to gossip and hear the news and pass the time away. Here again the make-believe Christians of this present age have assembled. Call it by any modern name: whether golf course, or ocean beach, or swimming-pool, or bridge club, or secret lodge, or theater, or house party, or wherever the children of this generation gather, there you will find make-believe Christians wasting instead of redeeming the time, frittering away the last precious hours of this dark age while the clock of God's Word ticks away relentlessly and the hands on the dial move close to midnight. Is it any wonder that such poor souls sit listlessly at church on Sunday morning, having ears but hearing not, having eyes but seeing not, having hearts but feeling not? For their minds are still out in the market-place and the public square where this poor, silly generation chatters away in a strife of tongues about the newest styles and the latest pictures and the freshest scandal. No man can be serious about the gospel and loiter in the emporium of this present age. His heart cannot blaze for God if he warms his heels by the enemy's fire in the courtyards of this passing world.

So these childish Christians *play at religion*. They join the church; they go to church; they work in the church, but they are only playing; it is not their life.

Just as these children of our Lord's time piped and mourned, played wedding and funeral, so these make-believe Christians pretend first to rejoice and then to weep. They sing with gusto:

> *Perfect submission, all is at rest,*
> *I in my Savior am happy and blest.*
> *Watching and waiting, looking above,*
> *Filled with His goodness, lost in His love;*
> *This is my story, this is my song,*
> *Praising my Savior all the day long.*

But they are neither submitted, happy, nor at rest, and as far as praising the Savior all the day long is concerned, when did they ever do that?

They turn around with equal ease to play funeral and to mourn. Their eyes well with tears at a sad story; they shake their heads soberly when the seriousness of the times is pictured, but it is only a pantomime; they go on living as they have always lived, pitying the victim by the wayside, but, like the Levite, passing by on the other side.

Even we orthodox and Bible-taught fundamentalists had better examine ourselves here. There is no sin more common, more deceptive, more disastrous, than the iniquity of pious make-believe. Indeed we can become so proficient at pretending that we deceive ourselves.

The actor seems real enough on the stage. If he is a good actor, he can so live the part that it is almost impossible to disentangle him from what he is portraying. He can so enter into the character of his subject, can so assume his peculiarities and manners, that he becomes identified with him. But when the show is over, the actor goes out the door himself, another man, leaving the character behind him. He is somebody else, you see, and he was only playing.

So, there is an imitation of Christ that is only a dramatic exhibition. It may repeat the holy phrases and recite His blessed word. It may assume His characteristics and practice His virtues until the face takes on a saintly look and the behavior becomes impressively other-worldly. Yet, for all that, it may be but the hollow pretense of those who call Him Lord, Lord, and do not what He commands.

It is an old story and well worn, of the minister who asked Macready, the actor, "Why do you draw out crowds to see you act while no one comes to hear me preach?" and he received the answer, "I act my fiction as though it were fact; you preach your facts as though they were fiction!" Nowhere is it easier to play with the gospel than in the ministry. With a pleasing personality, a gift of eloquence, a fine moral character, and plenty of business sense, one can take the gospel for a football and make a great many goals. But preaching is no game, and woe unto him who plays at it, whether he pipe or whether he mourn!

We remember David Hume's going to hear a very poor, plain preacher, and when asked why he attended such preaching when he did not believe it, answering: "I don't believe what he says, but he believes it, and once in a while I like to hear a man who believes what he says!" Our sinful generation sits unmoved today Sunday after Sunday before tasteless, dry, and powerless preaching because too often the minister himself is only reciting phrases that never have gripped him, just acting a part, an actor in a pulpit show.

God awaken us today to the awful sin of pious unreality! Just as we handle our coins and rarely examine them to see what is stamped thereon, so we handle the precious truths of the gospel and bandy about the spiritual coinage of our faith without stopping really to get acquainted with it and learn whose image and superscription are thereon. The holiness of God . . . we have heard of that all our lives, but have we ever fallen before Him broken and undone, crying, "Woe is me. . . . My comeliness is turned to corruption. . . . I am a sinful man, O Lord"?

The awfulness of sin . . . . we have dressed that nowadays in language of psychology; we have healed slightly our hurt and spread cold cream on cancer and blamed our evils on ancestors and environment. Sin is inhibited pleasure, arrested or incomplete development, biological growing-pains. We no longer weep for our transgression, because sin, as men now see it, is no longer anything to cry about. It is a plaything of the market-place.

The certainty of judgment .... who takes that seriously nowadays? "The wrath of God," "the terror of the Lord," "the lake of fire," . . . alas, hell has become the favorite byword of those who gather in the public square! Who shudders today to think of falling stars and burning worlds and multitudes at the great white throne when the books are opened? Who shrinks today from the horror of the undying worm and the fire unquenchable?

Calvary .... we sing about it, pay it tribute, but has the glory of Golgotha ever gripped our souls? Was it really at the cross, at the cross, where we first saw the light, and the burden of our hearts rolled away? Was it there by faith we received our sight, and now are we happy all the day?

The joy of salvation, the good cheer of sins forgiven — is it real or did we join a church on decision day with no sense of guilt removed, no experience of pardoning mercy? Spurgeon said, "He who has stood before God convicted and condemned with the rope around his neck .... is the man to weep with joy when he is pardoned and to live to the honor of his Redeemer by Whose blood he was cleansed." Was it grace that taught our hearts to fear and did grace our fears relieve? And just how precious did that grace appear the hour we first believed? Is the joy of the Lord our strength or do we merely pipe in the market-place?

The fire of Pentecost, the filling of the Spirit . . . how many today drunk on new wine, are beside themselves, are fools for Christ's sake? Is the holy flame real enough that we have become burning and shining lights, consumed with zeal for the house of God?

And what shall we say of the fellowship of the saints, the love of the brethren, which assures us that we have passed from death to life? The delights of the Word, the joy of service, the blessed hope of the Lord's return . . . . we are ready, you say? Yes, but are we expectant? How many of us have that hilarious abandon as pilgrims and strangers, citizens of heaven, joint-heirs with Christ, seeking a city to come? No wonder the early Christians shook the world. They did not play with the gospel; they took it seriously, and neither did they play with anything else. They really went to war; they did not stage a dress-parade with flag-wavings and drum-beatings and rattling of wooden swords. They endured hardness as good soldiers and did not entangle themselves with the affairs of this world. They were no children of the market-place just playing at religion in the courtyards of the age.

We live in an artificial day when the whole world has been turned into a public square. The auto and the radio have run us out of our last solitudes. The family cannot stay together long enough for prayer. Even the church has forgotten how to worship, and the hucksters of the market have been called in to run the business of God. We cannot escape the market-place today, but while we are in the world we need not be of it. If we must move in the public square, let us not go there as children to play. It is no easy thing to be a genuine Christian and take the gospel seriously before this unbelieving modern world. But if we are ever to glorify our God, we must learn that being a Christian is a life and not a play. We are not actors to imitate our Lord. The actor can impersonate his subject but he can never exchange his personality for the character he portrays. Here, however, we thank God that the analogy breaks down, for the believer may die to self, lose his own life, decrease that Christ may increase. Glorious reality that Christ lives again in His saints, who are not puppets on a stage but en-Christed souls who can exchange their lives for His and say, "For to me to live is Christ"; "Christ liveth in me." It is not imitation but identification and He will live again in any soul who will receive Him, yield to Him, trust and obey. He would not have us childish pretenders playing in the market-place. He would have us be converted and become as little children, genuine and true. God grant you may not be childish but child-like, Christ living in you.

V

WHAT IS A CHRISTIAN?

And the disciples were called Christians first at Antioch.
—ACTS 11:26

A LITTLE BOY asked his father, "What is a Christian?" The father explained to his son just what a Christian should be according to the Scriptures. But he told him so well that, when he had finished, the boy answered, "Father, have I ever seen a Christian?"

I have a real sympathy for that boy. In this befuddled age, when even the faithful are split by isms and schisms galore, one feels like rising in the midst of the bedlam to ask, "Just what is a Christian anyway?"

We have become so taken up with the things that accompany the Christian experience, the secondary matters, that the Christian himself can hardly be identified nowadays. The traveler has been lost in the baggage. One thinks of the housewife who answered the doorbell to be greeted by a stranger who abruptly asked, "Do you know Jesus Christ?" She was so taken aback that she could think of no answer and closed the door in his face. When she told her husband of it, he suggested, "But why didn't you tell him that you are president of the missionary society and teacher of the ladies' Bible class and active in all church work?" "But he didn't ask me about that," she replied; "he asked me *'Do you know Jesus Christ?'*" So, in the midst of the things we do and belong to, it is well to open the door on ourselves once in a while and ask abruptly, "What about you? For all your religious zeal and church work, *do you know Jesus Christ?*"

A Christian is one who knows the Lord Jesus Christ as a personal Savior and is living by faith in Him and in fellowship with Him. But we may go into detail and, to use the time-honored method of alliteration, put it thus:

First, a Christian is *saved*. "And the Lord added to the church daily such as should be saved" (Acts 2:47). It does not say "such as were sincere" or "such as were sanctimonious." The desire to build up an impressive church roll and send a pretentious letter to denominational headquarters has filled our churches with a strange assortment of saints and sinners, lost and saved. If the devil is pleased to see an unsaved man join the church—and he is—he ought to be happy today, for more are joining than ever before.

What is a true experience of salvation? There must be conviction of sin by the Spirit through the Word of God; conviction that we have sinned and come short of the glory of God, that we have broken God's law and are under condemnation, God's wrath abiding upon us. There must be repentance toward God, a change of mind about sin, self, and the Savior; godly sorrow for sin, turning with broken and contrite heart from sin to the Savior. There must be faith in the Lord Jesus Christ, faith that receives Him into the heart as the Son of God Who was made sin for us, Who bare our sins in His own body on the tree, Who rose for our justification, by Whose blood we are cleansed from sin, and through faith in Whom we are born again and receive power to become the sons of God. Then, belief with the heart must be followed by confession with the mouth, the public expression of an inward experience by which the redeemed of the Lord say so.

It is obvious that if all this is involved in an experience of salvation, it is miles away from perfunctorily signing a card or merely joining church. It is the most profound experience of human life when bondage turns to freedom, when darkness becomes day, when the angels of God are set singing because a sinner has come home.

In the second place, a Christian is not only saved but he should be *sure* that he is saved. A born-again, blood-washed believer has no right to go through this world a human question-mark, up one day and down the next, never able to stand at any time or place with full assurance of salvation. For the Word sets forth as plainly as day the blessed certainty of knowing Whom we have believed (II Tim. 1: 12): of knowing that we have eternal life (I John 5: 13); of knowing that He abides in us by the Spirit He has given us (I John 3: 24); of knowing that we have passed from death unto life because we love the brethren (I John

3: 14). The twice-born believer carries the evidences in that he is a new creature (II Cor. 5:17); he loves (I John 4: 7); he is not committing sin (I John 5: 18); and he overcomes the world (I John 5: 4). In a day of human question-marks every Christian should be a living exclamation-point bravely traveling through an uncertain world, knowing that he knows he is saved because God said so and God's saying so makes it so.

A Bible Christian is not only *saved* and *sure* but also *sound*. We are to be "sound in the faith" (Tit. 1:13), for we live in a day when men will not endure sound doctrine (II Tim. 4: 3). An aged woman who had a habit of using rather frequently the phrase "ner nuthin'," went to hear a Modernist preacher, who delivered a lavender and rose-water sermonette, starting nowhere and ending in the same place. After the service, she went forward to shake his hand and said, "I sure did enjoy yer sermon; it didn't have no doctrine in it — ner nuthin'." Certainly, if we have not sound doctrine, we have nothing!

It is a day of trumpets with uncertain sound. The less a preacher is sure of, the more intelligent some think him to be. It is true that we are saved by *Whom* we believe rather than *what*. But when the "whats" of doctrine deny the supernatural in the Whom, we have denied Christ Himself. We are witnesses unto Him, the Whom (Acts 1:8) but we are also witnesses of these things, the "whats" (Luke 24: 48). There is a great deal of pleasant teaching today to the effect that it matters not what we believe so long as we are all sincere and smiling, and we are paying for it in thousands of professing Christians who know little of what they believe and can give no reason for the hope within them. The blood makes *safe*, the Word makes *sure*, and as we continue steadfastly in the Apostles' doctrine, we are made *sound*, steadfast, immovable.

The next mark of a Bible Christian is that he is surrendered to God: "Yield yourselves unto God" (Rom. 6: 13). True victory begins with a surrender to the will of God. It has been pointed out that God required Abraham first to give up Ishmael, the worst thing in his life, born of the will of the flesh. He took Ishmael away, and he never came back. Then God asked for Isaac, the best thing in Abraham's life, born of faith. He gave Isaac back. So does God want the Ishmaels, the bad things in our lives, that He may take them away and they may never come back, and He wants the Isaacs, the best things, that He may sanctify them to His glory.

We need a day of national repentance for the way we sing songs in our churches we do not mean. It is perhaps easier to lie to music than in any other way. Consider how we sing:

> *My Jesus, I love Thee, I know Thou art mine,*
> *For Thee all the follies of sin I resign.*

Yet we have not resigned the follies of sin. We sing:

> *Have Thine own way, Lord, have Thine own way;*
> *Hold o'er my being absolute sway.*

Yet we have no intention of allowing God absolute sway. We sing:

> *Take my life and let it be . . . .*

And often that is just what we do mean—"Let it be; don't do anything with it, Lord; just take my life and let it be." We sing:

> *Take my hands and let them move*
> *At the impulse of Thy love.*

But who can imagine yielded hands playing cards? We sing:

> *Take my feet and let them be*
> *Swift and beautiful for Thee.*

But who can imagine yielded feet on a dance floor? We sing:

> *Take my voice and let me sing*
> *ALWAYS, ONLY, for my King.*

But who can imagine a yielded voice singing the silly songs of this world? And how easily do we sing:

> *Take my silver and my gold,*
> *Not a mite would I withhold.*

Yet we hold on to it with all our might!

Somewhere I have read of a child whose hand was caught fast in a glass vase. No one could understand how the hand went into the vase and would not come out. Finally, at great risk to the hand, they broke the vase and found that the hand was doubled in a little fist and there was a nickel in the fist! How often does God have to break us, our hearts, our lives, to make us surrender something worth less than a nickel!

A Bible Christian is not only *surrendered* but also *separated*. "Come out from among them, and be ye separate" (II Cor. 6: 17). The early Christians were a peculiar people; now we are a popular people. The early Christians were despised and derided outcasts from high society. Not many wise, mighty, or noble had been called. The world's interests and enthusiasms meant nothing to them. Paul and Peter could not have been found in an amphitheater watching a gladiatorial contest in the hope that their young people might be attracted by their broadmindedness to come to church. When the early Christians had anything to do with the frolics of heathenism, it was to be fed to lions or to be burned on a pole. Persecution failed to stop the church, but what persecution could not do popularity has almost done. It never was more fashionable to be a church-member than today and perhaps at no time has it meant less.

Christians are the light of the world, and our Lord suggested two simple things that can smother the light of our testimony: a bushel and a bed. The bushel stands for money-making, business cares, commercialism. The bed stands for luxury, ease, worldly pleasure. Most of our testimonies are either under the bushel or the bed. Most Christians are either too busy or too lazy to "let their light so shine." We are to have no fellowship with the unfruitful works of darkness, but rather reprove them (Eph. 5: 11). Mind you, it is not enough to let them alone; we must reprove them. We are to "abhor that which is evil" (Rom. 12: 9).

But separation is not merely a negative matter of "Don'ts." The Pharisees were separated and yet in their sins. It is not enough to be separated *from*; we must be separated *unto* the Lord. God wants ourselves, not merely the giving up of this evil or that. Peter forsook his boat and nets when first he followed the Lord, but it was three years later that he gave up Simon Peter. Sam Jones used to say: "I was going around with my pockets full of dirt when the Lord said, 'Sam, give up that dirt and I will fill your pockets with diamonds.' Who wouldn't give up dirt for diamonds?"

The Bible Christian is *Spirit-filled*. "Be filled with the Spirit" (Eph. 5:18). In the early church it was surprising to meet disciples who were *not* filled with the Spirit: today it is a surprise to meet one who *is*.

In the New Testament, wine and the Holy Spirit are connected in three different passages. John the Baptist was not to drink wine but be filled with the Spirit (Luke 1:15). The early Christians at Pentecost were accused of being drunk on new wine (Acts 2:13). And in Eph. 5:18 we are told, "Be not drunk with wine, wherein is excess; but be filled with the Spirit." There is a close parallel between the physical effect of wine and the spiritual effect of the Holy Ghost. Wine changes the face; so does the Spirit. The women of the country need their hearts lifted, not their faces. Wine changes the talk; the Spirit-filled man may not speak in an unknown tongue, but he will speak in a different tongue in that his conversation will be edifying and full of grace. Wine changes the walk; the Spirit-filled man walks a godly walk, worthy of his heavenly vocation. A man filled with wine creates a stir, and so does a Spirit-filled man follow in the steps of those early Christians who upset a world. The power of the Spirit is a stimulant, not a sedative.

Finally, a Bible Christian is a *singing* Christian. The same passage that tells us to be filled with the Spirit tells us to sing and make melody in our hearts to the Lord (Eph. 5: 19). God's statutes should be our songs in the house of our pilgrimage (Ps. 119: 54). The hallelujahs have gone from our churches. A popular prejudice against emotion has crowded our feelings out the back-door of our spiritual experiences. Emotions may be dangerous, but so is anything worth having. Man has intelligence, will, and emotions, and a genuine experience of grace will affect all three. We "sit on the lid" today and smother our joy until "amens" would not be scarcer if they cost ten dollars apiece. Finney said that there was no revival when Mr. Amen and Mr. Wet-Eyes could not be found in the audience.

I have read of a man who went to a coal-mine looking for a miner friend. They told him, "He's a singing Methodist, and if you hear somebody singing down there in the dark it will likely be your friend." Down into the earth he went, thinking, "If anybody is singing down here his song must be,

> *Down in a gulf of dark despair*
> *We wretched sinners lie."*

But presently he heard a voice, and the song was:

> *I've reached the land of corn and wine,*
> *And all its riches freely mine;*
> *Here shines undimmed one blissful day,*
> *And all my night has passed away!*

Yes, indeed; the grace of God puts a new song in our mouths, even praise unto our God!

These are the marks of a real Bible Christian: Saved, Sure, Sound, Surrendered, Spirit-filled, Singing. How many of the marks do you bear? Dr. Pace, the Christian cartoonist, spells it well when he makes it read: C-H-R-I-S-T- and I-A-N stands for I am Nothing. "To live is Christ!"

VI

NEEDED — A PROPHET

Covet earnestly the best gifts.—I Cor. 12: 31
Follow after love and desire spiritual gifts, but rather that ye may prophesy.—I Cor. 14: 1
He that prophesieth speaketh unto men to edification, and exhortation, and comfort.—I Cor. 14: 3

Since here is something that a Christian is allowed to covet, it deserves our careful attention. The New Testament prophet is not so much a foreteller as a forth-teller, carrying on a threefold ministry. His is a ministry of edification, a strengthening ministry; a ministry of exhortation, a stirring ministry; and a ministry of comfort, a soothing ministry. Bengel remarks: "The exhortation is to remove sluggishness and the comfort is to remove sadness!" As a minister of edification, he is a teacher; as a minister of exhortation, he is an evangelist; as a minister of comfort, he enters into the field of the pastor. Yet he is neither teacher, evangelist, nor pastor; he is a prophet!

Just now we are concerned, not so much with the work of the prophet itself, but with the need of a prophet. The work itself might interest only a few of us; the need concerns us all.

Consider first, the need of a ministry of edification, a strengthening ministry. Christians need to be built up in the Word today as never before. Our churches number thousands of members who, after years in the churches, are still babies in need of milk and who cannot bear meat; who ought to be teachers of the Word and need to be taught first principles. Some have plenty of zeal, far more of it than knowledge. They present the sad spectacle of a locomotive with plenty of steam but off the track and with only the whistle blowing, for the track is the Word of God and the best locomotives with most steam only end in the bog when they leave the charted course of "Thus saith the Lord."

We are not discrediting zeal. It is better to have more zeal than knowledge than to have more knowledge than zeal. It is better to run too fast than not to run at all, though one sometimes is reminded of the old church dignitary who was asked whether he thought a certain very enthusiastic sect of Christians would get to heaven. "Yes," he replied, "I think they will if they don't run past it."

Yet, for all that, one of the saddest mistakes a Christian ever makes is to try to live upon his experiences alone. More than one bases his hope on a "happy day that fixed his choice," forgetting that what gives that happy day its value is that the choice was fixed on "Him my Saviour and my God." Years ago I trusted Christ; but I am not depending upon my experience of Christ to save me; I am depending upon the Christ Who is greater than all our experiences. Thousands of Christians are wasting time and driving themselves into snares of the devil, chasing this experience and that instead of growing strong on the bread of God. It is possible even to substitute studying the Bible for feeding upon the Bible, analyzing what the Bible teaches without being vitalized by what the Bible says. A man might live in a bread shop and study calories and vitamins and starve: and just so may one divide and dissect the Scriptures and yet never be edified.

When I say "edified," I do not mean that comfortable, cozy feeling that comes over one after hearing a good sermon. Nothing is more disastrous than hearing good things without translating them into practice. Goethe said, "Thought without action is a disease," and many believers are so affected. We are not edified merely by hearing the Word. The Word does not profit us until it is mixed with faith in us who hear. We were bidden by our Lord to teach them *to observe* all the things commanded, and we have neither learned nor taught a truth until we have learned to put it into practice and have brought others to do so. We are not edified until the Word has been not only appreciated but appropriated; not only heard but heeded; not only adored but obeyed; for it is by reason of use that our senses are exercised to discern good and evil.

Consider, in the second place, the need of a ministry of exhortation, a stirring ministry. Isaiah lamented: "There is none that stirreth up himself to take hold of thee." Paul admonished Timothy to stir up the gift of God within him. If ever God's people needed to be awakened and aroused and shocked and alarmed into a sense of their holy privilege and solemn duty, it is today. "It is high time to awake out of sleep; for now is our salvation nearer than when we believed" (Rom. 13: 11).

Sometimes I have thought that the most unappreciated man on earth is a Pullman porter who must go down that mahogany lane in early morning to awaken passengers who are in no mood to be aroused. But this business of arousing people is a thankless job whether it apply to a Pullman porter at 6 A.M. or to a minister of the gospel at 11 A.M. Too many Christians come to church on Sunday to rest at ease in Zion and across their faces one seems to see as upon hotel room doors, "Please Do Not Disturb!"

It is not enough to be orthodox: we must awaken to action. We have more apologists than apostles. Too many fundamentalists are sound—sound asleep! Our theology needs to go up in doxology. We have the facts but not the fire. If we had as much vitality as we have had vocality, we would have set the world on fire long ago. We have talked much farther along than we have walked. We need to let our feet catch up with our tongues. We defend the truth, but we do not demonstrate the truth. We ponder it instead of proving it. We preach a dynamite gospel and live firecracker lives.

The power of the Holy Spirit is not a sedative but a stimulant. The early Christians were charged with being drunk on new wine. But the average Christian today seems more doped than drunk! To believe that we are living in the last days; that we are in the midst of a world of emergency; that judgment is just around the corner; that without Christ men are lost and sure for hell — to believe all that and then wend one's way complacently through a world of sin and shame is not merely unfortunate; it is criminal.

An infidel lawyer said to a young preacher who had come to interview him, "If I believed what you claim to believe, I could not take it as lightly as you do. I would not rest day nor night. I would warn men and plead with them to be saved. If I plead my cases like you present Christ, I would lose all of them."

Truly we need today a ministry of exhortation. Finney used to say, "We must have exciting and powerful preaching or the devil will have the people." We are interested, but only mildly interested, and this world has never been moved by mildly interested people. The saints who left their impression upon this poor world were men whom God made drunk and all the powers of Satan could not sober. If the gospel is not true, nothing matters; if it is true, nothing else matters. If it is not worth everything, it is not worth anything. Lincoln used to say that when he went to church, he wanted the preacher to preach as though he were fighting a swarm of bees. This generation is terribly excited about the unimportant and terribly unexcited about the important. The same church-members who yell like Comanche Indians at a football game sit like wooden Indians at church on Sunday. If ever Presbyterian sepulchers and Baptist graveyards and Methodist mausoleums are to resound with revival, we must recover the ministry of exhortation.

Finally, we need a ministry of comfort, a soothing

ministry. While most of us need stirring, many of us need to be calmed in our souls. "Comfort ye my people" is still the Word of the Lord. The world is living in a nervous breakdown; even the saints have the "jitters." The world is full of broken hearts. The journey is too great for them. They need to hear the Lord inviting the laboring and laden to His rest. They need to cease from their own works, to enter into rest, and study to be quiet and roll their burden on the Lord. They need a fresh experience of the Comforter; to wait on the Lord and increase their strength; to encourage themselves in the Lord their God. They need to learn that they have not received the spirit of bondage again to fear but that God has given them the spirit of love and of power and of a sound mind.

This poor, shell-shocked world tries to drown its misery in mirth and laugh away its pain, but one has only to look at the faces on the street to see that while they may wear gay robes without, they wear sackcloth next to their flesh.

Some time ago, a poor, nervous wreck called on a famous London doctor. Said the doctor, "You need to laugh. Go down to the theater and hear Grimaldi, that famous clown. All London is holding its sides laughing at him." But the visitor straightened himself and said, "Doctor, I am Grimaldi." No, we cannot laugh it off, but there is One whose cooling, healing touch has still its ancient power.

> *Jesus, the Name that charms our fears*
> *And bids our sorrows cease:*
> *'Tis music to the sinner's ear;*
> *'Tis life and health and peace.*

We need a ministry of comfort by which we may comfort others with the comfort wherewith we ourselves are comforted of God. We need men who have been to Gilead and have found a Physician there.

And what is the work of a prophet but simply to hold up Him Who, living within us, strengthens and stirs and soothes? Said Spurgeon: "In the days of Paul, the sum and substance of theology was Jesus Christ. I am not ashamed to vow myself a Calvinist. I do not hesitate to take the name of Baptist. But if I am asked what is my creed, I must reply, it is Jesus Christ."

That is the true theology of every prophet! "For we preach not ourselves but Christ Jesus the Lord; and ourselves your servants for Jesus' sake."

VII

"WHAT IS YOUR LIFE?"

In the book of James we are asked, "What is your life?" (4: 14). In Phil. 1: 21, Paul says, "For to me to live is Christ, and to die is gain."

In all seriousness, I would ask you, "What is your life?" You and I have been privileged to have a part in this adventure called living. What is it all about? What is the meaning of our existence? What is the true estimate of life?

There are those today who say that we came from nowhere and are going nowhere, who agree that life is but "a tale told by a fool, full of sound and fury, and signifying nothing." Life has been called "the predicament that precedes death," "a brief and discreditable episode on one of the minor planets." But there have always been those who, because they live in a cellar, never see the mountain-peaks; who, being deaf and blind, hear no music and see no meaning in our existence.

Then we have the university upstart who has been "on a four-year loaf and come home college bred," who "sees the price of everything and the value of nothing," with whom the human race is composed only of "small, crawling masses of impure carbohydrates, headed for oblivion." When these sophisticates speak lightly of God, one is reminded that in a wheat-field the heavy heads of wheat bend over and the empty one stands up straight; and when we see a head, young or old, that refuses to bow in His Presence, we reflect that it must be one of the empty ones that stands up straight.

But most of us are in our right minds; we do not believe that this universe is but a concourse of eighty-odd chemical elements, the joke of a meaningless fate. We believe that "life is real, life is earnest, and the grave is not the goal."

Paul said, "For to me to live is Christ." For you to live is — what?

There are three false estimates of life. Sometimes I call them, "The Three T's." First, there is *things*. There are those who live for things, but that is a mistake, for "a man's life consisteth not in the abundance of the things which he possesseth" (Luke 12:15). The leading business in America is the junk business. We do not call it junk today; it is cars and clothes and finery and furnishings; but tomorrow it is rusty or moth-eaten, for men still lay up their treasures on earth where moth and rust corrupt and where thieves break through and steal.

I heard William Jennings Bryan say: "Those who live for money spend the first half of their lives getting all they can from everybody else and the last half trying to keep everybody else from getting what they have got away from them, and they find no pleasure in either half." I have heard that someone asked Mr. Rockefeller, "How much money does it take to satisfy a man?" He answered, "Just a little more." As small a thing as a penny will shut out from our vision as large a thing as the sun, and so does as small a thing as money shut out God.

I have read of a man who was found dead in a desert. He had strapped around him precious stones worth thousands of dollars, but he died for lack of plain drinking water — something absolutely free. So do men die with plenty around them, plenty of this world's goods strapped to them, but they die spiritually for want of the water of life, which is given freely without money and without price. Such is the tragedy of those who lay up treasure for themselves but are not rich toward God.

Paul speaks of "having nothing, yet possessing all things." It is the Christian's paradox. "All things are yours," says the Word to the believers; all things except yourself: "Ye are Christ's, and Christ is God's." We are not our own; we are bought with a price.

So we are not to live for things, but if we seek first the kingdom of God and His righteousness, all needed things will be added. What we eat and drink and wear, the world makes these things a business; with the Christian they are only by-products. In these days when men spend their health looking for wealth and then spend their wealth looking for health, we need to remember John's word to Gaius: "I wish in all things that thou mayest prosper and be in health even as thy soul prospereth." God wants no man to be richer than his soul. Therefore, things are not life's true estimate, for we are to look to the unseen, not the seen; for things seen are temporal, but the things not seen are eternal.

Then there are those whose estimate of life is found in *thrills*. But God's Word says, "She that liveth in pleasure is dead while she liveth" (I Tim. 5:6). Since that is true, then there certainly are a lot of animated corpses running around nowadays!

A colored man, alighting from a merry-go-round, was met by his wife with this accusation: "Now, look at you; you spent your money, you got off right where you got on, and you ain't been nowhere!" It is a good description of modern living, a senseless whirl, which has been spelled in three words—Hurry, Worry, Bury. Millions live for pleasure and never have it because they make it a business, whereas it is a by-product. The most miserable poor mortals on earth are those who scurry around in automobiles looking for a good time and never find it, who argue that "variety is the spice of life" and don't have sense enough to know that we can't live on spice. These thrill-chasers speak of the gospel as an opiate, something for children and old people. Imagine such ice-cream-soda characters with ukelele souls trying to keep step with Paul and Savonarola and Wesley and Moody! Such poor, deluded pleasure-hunters know nothing of the real thrills of following Christ.

Why should we frequent the lunch-counters of earthly pleasure when we have standing invitations to the banquet of the grace of God? There are two kinds of pleasure: "She that liveth in pleasure is dead while she liveth" and "At thy right hand there are pleasures forevermore" (Ps. 16: 11). Seek the thrills that God gives, "joy unspeakable and full of glory." "The blessing of the Lord, it maketh rich, and he addeth no sorrow with it" (Prov. 10: 22). There is no morning-after taste to the joy of the Lord!

Again there are those who would estimate life in terms of *theories*. "The world by wisdom knew not God" (I Cor. 1: 21). Josh Billings used to say, "I'd rather know a few things for certain than be sure of a lot of things that ain't so." We try to go head first when God's way is heart first. We cannot educate ourselves into life's true estimate, for while education may change the size, it doesn't change the sort.

A phrenologist was giving an exhibition, calling various members of his audience to the platform, feeling the bumps on their heads, then describing them to the listeners. He called forward one man who had been a man of evil reputation in days past but who had been saved by the grace of God and had for years lived a consistent Christian life. The phrenologist, knowing only his way of sizing up the man, proceeded after his examination to describe to the audience the man as he used to be, but everybody smiled because they knew the description no longer held true. Finally, the man himself stood and said, "Professor, you are telling them the kind of man I used to be. Since then, the Lord Jesus Christ has come into my life and now, if you size me up correctly, you'll have to come from my head down to my heart, for the Lord lives there."

Men try to find their way through the puzzle of life with the candle of reason and do not realize that God has kept these things from the wise and prudent and has revealed them to babes. Men hunt through libraries for truth while perhaps the janitor sweeping the steps has found it long since in Jesus Christ.

Sometimes I am much amused reading modern "Open Sesames" to health, wealth, and happiness, the latest isms and fads, treatises on the subconscious that read as though they were written by someone who was unconscious when he wrote them! Of course there is some truth in all of it: we have an old clock at home that won't run, and it is right two times every day!

A doctor friend of mine gave me a book composed of the statements of faith, or rather of the lack of faith, of many prominent writers. I read it awhile and was growing rather weary of it when the radio began to broadcast from somewhere those precious lines of that great hymn:

> *Change and decay in all around I see;*
> *O Thou Who changest not, abide with me.*

I threw down the book and said, "Thank God, I don't have to read such guesswork. 'I *know* whom I have believed, and am persuaded that he is able to keep that which I have committed unto him against that day' " (II Tim. 1:12). "If any man will do his will, he shall know the doctrine" (John 7:17). "Ye shall *know* the truth, and the truth shall make you free" (John 8:32). "We *know* that we have passed from death unto life, because we love the brethren" (I John 3:14). "We *know* that all things work together for good to them that love God, to them who are the called according to his purpose" (Rom. 8: 28). "We *know* that if our earthly house of this tabernacle were dissolved, we have a building of God, an house not made with hands, eternal in the heavens" (II Cor. 5:1).

If life's true valuation is not to be found in things, thrills, and theories, then where shall we look? The other way is the way of truth. Our Lord, on trial before Pilate, said, "My kingdom is not of this world [that is, it is not a kingdom of things, thrills, and theories]: . . . To this end was I born, and for this cause came I into the world, that I should bear witness unto the truth. Everyone that is of the truth heareth my voice" (John 18: 36-37). Pilate asked wearily, "What is truth?" Men still are asking, "What is truth?" but truth is a Whom: Christ is the truth, not merely a truth-teller, and when Paul said, "For me to live is Christ," he was giving us life's true estimate. It is not to live *for* Christ or *like* Christ, mind you, but to live *is* Christ.

Christ was everything to Paul. He was the source of Paul's life: "I give unto them eternal life." He was the sustenance of Paul's life: "To live *is* Christ." Paul had no plans, ambitions, purposes of his own. He was not merely trying to live like Christ. Christ was living His life in Paul. And that is life; not that we merely make Christ our ideal, but that He through regeneration enters our broken lives to live His life in us. It is not His purpose to improve or reform us but to have full control over our yielded wills, to increase while we decrease. It is not inspiration or imitation but identification: "To live is Christ."

It has been pointed out that here we also have the true estimate of death: "To die is gain." We must first say, "To live is Christ," before we can say, "To die is gain." We cannot say, "To live is money and to die is gain." It fits nothing but Paul's statement. We must have his estimate of life to have his estimate of death. And when we do, even death becomes a paying proposition: "To depart and be with Christ is far better."

What is your life? Are you forever blowing bubbles, looking for ships that never come in, chasing pots of gold at the end of vanishing rainbows? Have you read many books and found them a weariness of the flesh? Have you built your castles and had them tumble about your ears in ruins? You never can find life until you find it in Christ, for He is THE LIFE.

A little girl had torn up a map of the United States and was trying to put it back together. But Maine would be right beside Montana and Indiana beside Oregon, and she was almost ready to give up when she remembered that on the reverse side of the map there was a picture of George Washington. She did know what he looked like, so when she had assembled that side, she had the other also.

Life without Christ is a hopeless jigsaw puzzle. But when we know Him and see His face, all else fits together, for "by Him all things consist." "To live *is* Christ." "What is *your* life?"

VIII

"AND HE STOOD SPEECHLESS"

In the first fourteen verses of the twenty-second chapter of Matthew, our Lord gives a parable setting forth God's dealings with man concerning salvation from the very beginning. The story of the wedding feast is unusual in that it combines past history with future prophecy. Some of it has already taken place; more of it is happening before our eyes; and the rest is sure to come.

"The kingdom of heaven is like unto a certain king, which made a marriage for His son." The King is God, Who prepares a wedding supper for His Son, Jesus Christ, and His Son's bride, the church. The Jews were familiar with the Old Testament figure of Jehovah and His wife, Israel, long since become adulterous. Now a new figure arises to picture the union of Christ with believers. Paul wrote of having espoused the Corinthian Christians unto one husband, the risen Lord. Then there is the beautiful passage in Eph. 5: 22-32, using the marriage relationship to illustrate the same truth.

This marriage reaches its heavenly consummation at the marriage supper of the Lamb described in Rev.

19: 7-9, where the bride is arrayed in fine linen, clean and white, the righteousness of the saints — a detail we should remember in connection with this parable.

"And sent forth his servants to call them that were bidden to the wedding: and they would not come." The servants here are all the prophets from Moses to John the Baptist, inviting Israel. But they would not come, and our Lord lamented as He wept over Jerusalem that He would have gathered them but they would not.

"Again, he sent forth other servants, saying, Tell them which are bidden, Behold, I have prepared my dinner: my oxen and my fatlings are killed, and all things are ready: come unto the marriage" (Matt. 22:4). Between verses 3 and 4, Christ has come, has died, and has risen, and all things are ready. The bread of life, the water of life, the Passover Lamb, all are ready, the gracious provisions of the gospel are spread, and the servants, the early Apostles and witnesses, go out to invite the Jews again. Peter preached on Pentecost to a Jewish audience.

"But they made light of it, and went their ways, one to his farm, another to his merchandise." This reminds us of those in Luke 14: 18-20, who had bought land and oxen and married and could not come. This crowd was not hostile, just preoccupied. In the days of Lot they did eat and drink, they bought and sold, they planted and builded, and most people today miss heaven because they are taken up with things perhaps not evil in themselves, but secondary interests that keep them from God's best. These invited guests excused themselves, and so do men today offer silly arguments to explain why they prefer to go to hell. There are no reasons, only excuses, and an excuse is but the skin of a reason stuffed with a lie. "They went their ways" and so have we "turned every one to his own way." But the wicked must "forsake his way if he is to be saved" (Isa. 55: 7).

"And the remnant took his servants, and entreated them spitefully, and slew them." The Jewish rulers persecuted the early witnesses, slew Stephen and James.

"But when the king heard thereof, he was wroth: and he sent forth his armies, and destroyed those murderers, and burned up their city." This is ancient history. God was angry and sent the Roman armies, His armies in the sense that they were the instruments of His anger as was the Assyrian in Isa. 10: 5, to destroy Jerusalem. Jesus prophesied it clearly, and it came literally to pass in the slaughter of over a million Jews and the demolishing of their city. Truly, their house was left unto them desolate.

"Then saith he to his servants, The wedding is ready, but they which were bidden were not worthy. Go ye therefore into the highways, and as many as ye shall find, bid to the marriage." The gospel preachers went forth from then unto now into the highways and hedges to compel them to come in. We are debtors to everyone, the progressive throngs on the highways, the poor and despised in the hedges. We are to compel them with the compulsion of urgent love, snatching some from the fire, for it is a day of good tidings, and we do not well to hold our peace. The objective is that His house may be filled, and when His elect number is gathered, He will come.

"So those servants went out into the highways, and gathered together all as many as they found, both bad and good: and the wedding was furnished with guests." Into the professing church will come both the true and the false. The minister has no way of reading hearts, but "the Lord knoweth them that are his." Just as the net gathered good fish and bad (Matt. 13: 47-50) so do soul-winners gather into the professing church both true possessors and mere professors. Many are called with the general gospel calling, but not many are chosen, not many belong to the effectual calling of Rom. 8: 30; not many truly receive Christ and are born again.

But now I come to the climax of this parable, and the part with which I am most concerned just now: "And when the king came in to see the guests, he saw there a man which had not on a wedding garment." Our Lord seems to have in mind a passage from Zephaniah: "Hold thy peace at the presence of the Lord God: for the day of the Lord is at hand: for the Lord hath prepared a sacrifice, he hath bid his guests. And it shall come to pass in the day of the Lord's sacrifice, that I will punish the princes, and the king's children, and all such as are clothed with strange apparel" (1: 7, 8).

I have heard many sermons on the man who bought land, the man who bought oxen, the man who married a wife and could not come. I have never heard a sermon on the man who came and yet went to hell.

This man offered no excuses; he did not persecute the servants. He *came*, yet he was cast out as though he had bitterly opposed the whole matter. What was the reason? I read that the king "saith unto him, Friend, how camest thou in hither not having a wedding garment? And he was speechless."

Why was he speechless? Maybe he had not heard that a certain garment must be worn. Maybe he was not able to secure one or perhaps he did not have time. But we are told that on such occasions the host provided wedding garments, which were put on when the guests arrived; so there was no excuse.

There are thousands in our churches today called but not chosen. They appear righteous before men, but they wear not the wedding garment of the righteousness of Christ. "I will greatly rejoice in the Lord, my soul shall be joyful in my God; for he hath clothed me with the garments of salvation, he hath covered me with the robe of righteousness, as a bridegroom decketh himself with ornaments, and as a bride adorneth herself with her jewels" (Isa. 61: 10). "Our righteousnesses are as filthy rags" (Isa. 64: 6) but the Lord Jesus Christ is made unto us righteousness (I Cor. 1: 30) and we are to put on the Lord Jesus Christ and make no provision for the flesh (Rom. 13: 14).

You may hear and answer the general gospel invitation; you may go to church, belong to a church, pray in the church, pay to the church, be active in a church; but if you are not robed in the righteousness of Christ Himself, the wedding garment the King provides, you will stand on that day condemned, hearing the King say, "How camest thou in hither?" It is only as we are "clad in His righteousness alone" that we are "faultless to stand before the throne."

"And he was speechless." The word really is "muzzled." Men can talk aplenty now; we run into many long-winded and loud-mouthed individuals who can talk like phonographs as they try to justify themselves, but there will come a day when their little speech will not do; they will stand muzzled before the King.

"Then said the king to his servants, Bind him hand and foot, and take him away, and cast him into outer darkness; there shall be weeping and gnashing of teeth." God commands the angels not only to cast the offender into outer darkness but first—and we read of it nowhere else—to bind him hand and foot. Mind you, it is the Lord Jesus Himself who gives us this awful detail. We seem to forget that the most fearful pictures of future punishment recorded in the Bible come to us from the Lord Jesus Himself.

"For many are called, but few are chosen." Many are basing their hopes on an external call instead of upon an eternal choice. Many are called, but only those who accept the righteousness of God and put on the Lord Jesus Christ and are thus made the righteousness of God in Him, only these pass inspection before the King. All others are but spots in the feasts (Jude 12). Then let us give diligence to make our calling and election sure (II Pet. 1:10) lest after living in a church all our lives, we end in outer darkness. "Examine yourselves, whether ye be in the faith" (II Cor. 13:5). "Put on the Lord Jesus Christ"!

IX

"ENTERED INTO REST"

Often in strolling through cemeteries we have come upon the inscription, "Entered into Rest." It tells us that some soul has moved out from earth's sorrow and struggle, some traveler gone home evermore to be with the Lord.

Precious indeed is that assurance offered in God's Word for all who believe on the Lord Jesus Christ. But the believer need not wait until he reaches the grave to enter the Christian's rest. "There remaineth a rest to the people of God," but although heaven is its consummation and perfection, it need not begin there. Just as there is a love of God and peace of God and joy of the Lord, there is a rest of God, and it is open here and now in this present life to whomsoever will enter in.

Certainly ours is a restless world today. "There is no peace, saith the Lord, unto the wicked" (Isa. 48:22). "The wicked are like the troubled sea, when it cannot rest, whose waters cast up mire and dirt" (Isa. 57: 20). Men dope themselves with the sedatives of sin and get drunk on all the stimulants of Satan, but they awake more wretched than ever.

Even Christians who claim to have anchored their souls in the haven of rest allow fear and doubt and worry to rob them of their blessed privileges in Christ. They live in a strain, taking their spiritual pulse and temperature, wearing themselves out in flesh effort, tense and feverish. This is not God's way, for He is neither hurried nor worried. Such Christians have not entered into rest.

In the midst of all the turmoil, our Lord invites us to His rest (Matt. 11: 25-30). First, He states the simplicity of it: "I thank thee, O Father, Lord of heaven and earth, because thou hast hid these things from the wise and prudent, and hast revealed them unto babes. Even so, Father: for so it seemed good in thy sight." Not many wise, mighty, noble have been called. While the worldly wise and the sophisticated stumble around looking for something complex and elaborate, the simple and child-hearted enter into rest. Only children and the child-hearted are genuine: all others are clowns.

Then the Lord declares the sublimity of this rest; He shows us His resources. "All things are delivered unto me of my Father: and no man knoweth the Son, but the Father; neither knoweth any man the Father, save the Son, and he to whomsoever the Son will reveal him." All good things come from God (James 1: 17); all has been given the Son by the Father; and all things belong to the believer (I Cor. 3: 21). It is God's own rest given to us in Christ.

The Lord Jesus then gives us the secret of this rest: "Come unto me, all ye that labor and are heavy laden, and I will give you rest. Take my yoke upon you, and learn of me; for I am meek and lowly in heart: and ye shall find rest unto your souls. For my yoke is easy, and my burden is light." He invites the laboring and the laden. Men labor today in a vicious circle, "getting on" without stopping to ask, "On where?" And men are laden today, burdened with loads no mortal can carry at this terrific modern pace. Suicide, crime, insanity, heart failures, physical collapse, all declare that the journey is too great. They try to flee as a bird to this and that mountain. They seek surcease in this fad and that ism, in wine and carousing. They steel themselves in hard-boiled cynicism or try to laugh it off in bitter nonchalance. But the burden grows heavier, and then they seek rest in the grave. Alas, the grave will bring no rest, for it takes more than a shroud and casket to give peace to the soul!

The only way out is to come to the Lord Jesus Christ, Who gives rest. But He also says we are to learn of Him and find rest. His rest is both an obtainment and an attainment. The possession involves a process. When we come to the Saviour, receive Him into the heart, we have peace with God through our Lord Jesus Christ. Christ is ours, and all that is His becomes ours, including His rest. Then, as we abide in Him, walk in the light, learn of Him, we find rest; we realize rest in actual daily experience; the peace of God garrisons our hearts and minds through Christ Jesus. Thus we might say the rest He gives is the believer's by virtue of his new *position*; the rest we learn is realized in the believer's *practice*. Because we have the possession, we must not ignore the process. There is nothing to earn but much to learn. All things are ours, but we must take His yoke upon us and become His disciples; we must let His mind be in us; we must put on the Lord Jesus Christ.

But His yoke is easy, and His burden is light. It is the yoke of bondage and the unequal yoke that crush the soul. Too many think of our Lord's yoke as an extra load in addition to what we already carry. But it is wings, not weights. By it all other loads are lightened. We cast all our care upon Him Who cares for us. His statutes become our songs in the house of our pilgrimage. If we know these things, *happy* are we if we do them. Too many think only of rules and responsibility, but what He offers us is *rest!*

Turning to Heb. 4: 1-11, we learn more of the believer's rest. It is typified by the Promised Land and the Sabbath rest of God after the finished creation. The Israelites did not follow Joshua into the land and so missed what God had prepared for them. Canaan represents a happy Christian life and not heaven as so many who sing, "I Am Bound for the Promised Land," wrongly imagine. We have no business standing on Jordan's stormy banks casting a wishful eye toward Canaan's fair and happy land where our possessions lie. We are to enter and possess and eat the fruit of the land; not live on samples brought back by spies.

Heaven is, indeed, the perfect and complete rest of the believer, but there remains a rest to the people of

God here and now in this present life for all who will cross Jordan and follow the New Testament Joshua, Jesus, the Captain of our salvation, in spiritual conquest. Just as God rested from creation on the seventh day, so the believer rests in a perfect redemption. "He that is entered into his rest, he also hath ceased from his own works, as God did from his." It is hard to learn that God has wrought in Christ all that is necessary for our salvation and sanctification and every other need, and we have but to "let go and let God." Just as one cannot sleep so long as he lies in nervous tension, "trying to hold up the bed," so we cannot rest until we learn to relax spiritually and cast all our cares upon Him who cares for us.

We are exhorted, "Let us labor therefore to enter into that rest." That is, we are to apply ourselves diligently to learn this secret and enter into it. It certainly is worth giving one's earnest thought to. We ought to make it our business until we have learned it, for although it is not earned, it is learned as we take our Lord's yoke upon us and become His disciples. But just here comes a difficulty. We imagine that this rest is so complicated only a few can reach up to it, whereas it is so simple that only a few get down to it. The very simplicity of it seems to hide it from those who look for the complex and elaborate. The whole matter is just one of believing that God has said and done enough to rest upon it in childlike confidence. Many dear souls just cannot believe that it can be as simple as that!

What is it to enter into this rest? To rest in Him

for salvation is simply to depend upon His finished work on Calvary without any works of our own. Surely if God is satisfied with our Lord's accomplished salvation, we ought to be! To rest in Him for assurance is to believe we are saved because God's Word declares it. To rest in Him for sanctification is to accept and receive and trust Christ within us as our righteousness, made unto us sanctification. To rest in Him for power is to ask for and receive by faith the fulness of the Spirit, then, believing we have received, to go forth to serve and testify, reckoning on the Power where and when we need it. We rest in Him for every need of spirit, mind, and body because He has promised to supply them and to make all grace abound toward us. We rest in Him for the future because He has promised we shall be with Him.

We know these facts and promises, but according to our faith really to believe them shall it be unto us. We confuse the whole matter trying to explain it. Here the simple soul finds peace while scholars wear themselves out trying to unravel it. We enter into His rest the day we really let go our tense and nervous strain and rest upon His Word, however unreal it may appear. There is no other way. It is not a matter of vision, strange feelings, emotional ecstasies. It is as definite as walking through an open doorway. We labor to enter into rest only in bringing ourselves to where we give up trying to understand it and reason it away and simply trust and obey. There may be at first a "sinking feeling" as though we had stepped out upon air, but we shall find the Rock beneath our feet.

We read of a man walking along a steep precipice at night. Slipping, he fell over what he thought was the edge of the cliff. Grasping a shrub, he held on tensely until his grip failed him and he fell — just six inches to solid ground beneath his feet! So we hold onto this or that until strength fails us and we let go and find God.

This way the saints of the ages have gone. From the fever of the seventh chapter of Romans Paul entered the rest of the Spirit-filled life. After dissatisfied years, George Fox entered that rest when, as he put it, "I saw into that which was without end, and things which cannot be uttered, and of the greatness and infinitude of the love of God, which cannot be expressed by words." John Bunyan groped in soul-turmoil of dreadful doubts and fears until one day while crossing a field he was set free by the words, "Thy righteousness is in heaven." John Wesley, after ten years seeking peace and rest, crossed into Canaan when, to use his words, "In the evening I went very unwilling to a society in Aldersgate Street, where one was reading Luther's preface to the Romans. About a quarter before nine, while he was describing the change God works in the heart through faith in Christ, I felt my heart strangely warmed. I felt I did trust in Christ alone for salvation; and an assurance was given me that He had taken away my sins, even mine, and saved me from the law of sin and death."

Well might Wesley receive help from Martin Luther,

for it was that giant of God who, as an emaciated monk, worn out with trying to earn his own salvation, learned one happy day as he read that liberating message of Romans that "a man is justified by faith without the deeds of the law." No longer enslaved in hopeless bondage of flesh effort that can never do enough to claim forgiveness, that day he crossed Jordan to thunder through the ages the glorious gospel: "By grace are ye saved through faith and that not of yourselves; it is the gift of God."

It was George Whitefield who wandered around Kadesh-Barnea seeking rest through asceticism, fastings, and countless austerities, living on tea and bread until his frail body could scarcely climb the stairs. Nor did rest ever come until he got his eyes off himself and upon the Saviour and was able to say, "Oh, with what joy, joy unspeakable, even joy that was full of and big with glory, was my soul filled, when the weight of sin went off and an abiding sense of the pardoning love of God and a full assurance of faith broke in upon my disconsolate soul."

It was that saint, John Fletcher, who wearied himself at all hours of the night in quest of peace, drawing up resolutions, sinning and repenting, sinning and repenting, until one dreary day, tired and despondent, his eye fell at last upon that sign-post that points to rest: "Cast thy burden upon the Lord, and he shall sustain thee"! And then and there another troubled soul moved out of the feverish grind of self-effort into the Sabbath of His rest.

What more shall we say? One thinks of A. B. Earle,

the Spirit-filled evangelist, with a heart ill at ease for years, until one day a sweet, heavenly peace filled his soul, and a calm, simple, childlike trust took possession of his whole being. One thinks of Frances Ridley Havergal wrestling with sin and worn out with heart-searching until that blessed word of I John 1: 7, "The blood of Jesus Christ his Son *cleanseth* us from all sin," proved the key that unlocked the gates of bondage to set her free. Catherine Booth, exhausted with a day of praying, lay on a sofa to rest and found there the rest of faith as she realized that whatsoever toucheth the altar is most holy and that if all is on the altar, all is holy. Phoebe Palmer after seeking long and earnestly for peace because she thought it could only be reached through agony and struggle, learned it is found not by wrestling but by clinging and that "when she gave all trying over, simply trusting, she was blessed."

In these insane, terrific days, when the journey is too great for us all, may we come to our Lord and receive His rest; take His yoke upon us and find rest; labor to enter into rest; leave the wretched wilderness wanderings and possess the land; abandon frantic strivings of the flesh and cease from our own works as God did from His.

X

WHERE ARE YOU AT CALVARY?

IN our thought, let us go back to a little hill called Calvary and look on an old rugged cross, the emblem of suffering and shame. And as we survey the wondrous cross on which the Prince of Glory died, I trust we shall count our richest gain but loss and pour contempt on all our pride. As we gather around Golgotha to visualize afresh that tragedy that marked the crossroads of the ages, let us remember that each of us is represented in one or another of the groups that met at the cross. It seems that God so arranged it that every sort of man or woman is typified in the different classes that watched Him die.

The Negroes have a song, "Were You There When They Crucified My Lord?" Yes, you were there, you *are* there, for Calvary stands in the midst of the swarming multitudes today. There is a sense in which you stand at Calvary now, and your condition is declared, your salvation is decided, your destiny is determined, by the attitude you take toward the cross of Christ and the Christ of the cross.

WHERE ARE YOU AT CALVARY? 87

Study the groups that gathered at Calvary, and see if you can find your crowd there. Consider first the soldiers. They clad Him in the robe; they spat in His face; they pressed the crown of thorns upon His brow and watched the blood and spittle mix upon His face; they smote Him and mocked Him and nailed Him to the tree. But they only administered the wounds that all the sin of all the world had caused. It was you and I who spat upon Him, who crowned Him with the thorny diadem. Your sins and mine nailed Him to the tree. We had a part in that, for "He was wounded for *our* transgressions. He was bruised for *our* iniquities; the chastisement of *our* peace was upon him; and with *his* stripes *we* are healed. All *we* like sheep have gone astray; *we* have turned every one to his own way; and the Lord hath laid on him the iniquity of *us* all."

When you refuse Him, when you live on in sin and spurn the Word and reject the pleading of the Spirit, you are pressing the thorny crown upon Him, you are spitting upon Him, smiting Him, crucifying Him. You cannot blame it on the soldiers; you are more guilty than they. He said they knew not what they did, but you know: you live in a land of Bibles and churches. I had rather have been that ignorant Roman soldier than an intelligent American now if I were determined to reject Him.

We read further of these soldiers that "sitting down, they watched him there" (Matt. 27: 36). As you read this message presenting Christ crucified, you also "sit and watch Him there." And although you helped to put Him there and are more guilty than the soldiers, you do not seem to care. How can men's hearts be so hard? How can they watch Him there in sermon and song and yet politely go away as though it made no difference that He lived or died?

The soldiers also gambled for the seamless robe (John 19: 23-24). It was bad enough to watch, but they gambled, and for His vestments they cast lots! The world plays its games today at the foot of the cross. No matter where you are, you are facing Calvary, and men sit before the eternal fact and gamble away health and time and talents and reputation and soul while the crucified Christ looks on. It matters not what else you are, if you are not a "soldier OF the cross" you are a soldier AT the cross, gambling away your day of grace, gambling for money and pleasure and position and the tinsel trinkets of earth. And soon you must pass away and other gamblers take your place, while you move out into darkness, for the cross will have sentenced you: "He that believeth not is condemned already." Are you a soldier at the cross?

We read next of those who "passed by, wagging their heads" (Matt. 27: 39-40; Mark 15: 29-30). These passers-by did not actually crucify Him; they only passed by, reviling Him. It is fashionable nowadays to pass by Calvary, wagging the head. From the blasphemers of Russia to indifferent souls who use the name of Jesus as a by-word, men pass by the cross today and jeer at the Prince of Glory.

The Word records three things of these passers-by. First, they misquoted the claims of our Lord. They shouted, "Thou that destroyest the temple, and buildest it in three days, save thyself." He had not said that; He had said, "Destroy this temple, and in three days I will raise it up" (John 2: 19). But that is as near as critics ever come to the truth! What a perfect type of those who twist the Scriptures to suit their own purposes!

Then, they minimized His death. "Save thyself; come down from the cross." They did not believe He "must needs have suffered" or that "He that saveth his life shall lose it." So modern critics make light of Calvary, see no need for atonement, ridicule a "slaughter-house theology." It is the same old philosophy of "save thyself" that would bring Christ down from the cross, because to them His death was unnecessary.

Finally, the passers-by mocked His Deity. "If thou be the Son of God, come down from the cross." But that was exactly what kept Him on the cross! Today critics wag their heads and deny His deity and speak of the peril of worshiping Jesus. They reduce His holy name "Emmanuel" to mere "man"; they see a great teacher, an idealist, the crystal Christ but not the Calvary Christ. The first word of their creed is "If," just as these passers-by cast their doubts at Him: "If thou be the Son of God . . . ."

Are you among the passers-by, wagging your head at Calvary? Do you misquote His claims and twist the Scriptures to suit yourself? Do you minimize His death and whittle down the meaning of the cross? Do you doubt His deity and see in His death only a noble example of self-sacrifice? It is a dreadful thing to be a passer-by at Calvary!

Consider a third group at the cross, the chief priests, scribes, and elders (Matt. 27: 41-43). Here is the religious class! One would have expected them to be quiet and dignified at least, but even the sanctimonious chief priests forgot themselves and cried with the rabble. Alas, no group of men behaved worse at the cross than the religionists. Who were these men who stood at Calvary and taunted the Son of God? Men who studied the Scriptures, prayed in public, attended the house of God, gave tithes, led clean moral lives; but for all that they joined the enemies of Christ at Calvary. Today there are no worse enemies of the Lord Jesus than those hypocrites whose names are on the church books, who work in the church, read the Bible, pray in public, give their money to the church, but for all that, "draw near with their mouths and honor with their lips but their hearts are far from Him." No group of men and women has caused more pain to the heart of Christ than the Pharisees, who go through all the motions of Christianity, sing its hymns and recite its creeds and keep its ordinances, but never come under the blood of the cross in a genuine experience of saving faith. No matter what else they may do, their lives are a hollow mockery; they stand with the priests, scribes, and elders at Calvary.

Another group stood at the cross—the general crowd termed simply "the people." "And the people stood beholding. . . . And all the people that came together to that sight, beholding the things which were done, smote their breasts, and returned" (Luke 23: 35, 48). They did not revile, nor wag their heads; they just looked and did nothing. Most people come under this classification: When Christ is preached and the cross is held up, they do not revile nor insult the Lord; they just look on respectfully and then do nothing about it. But all that any man need to do to be lost is just . . . nothing. "How shall we escape if we *neglect* so great salvation?" and to neglect one need do nothing at all. It is not necessary to be a drunkard, a thief, or an infidel. One need only "stand beholding," listen to sermons, pay polite attention, and let it go at that, and he will find himself as truly lost as the worst criminal. Looking unto Jesus will save us, but merely looking at Jesus has never saved anyone and never will. These people behold Him; they looked *at* Him but not *unto* Him.

It is added that "they smote their breasts and returned." It is possible to go a step farther than beholding Him and still be lost. These people were impressed at Calvary; the darkness and the death of the Lord stirred them; and the awful solemnity of the greatest hour in history hushed them with an awful silence. But they only smote their breasts and went away. So do men sit under the preaching of the gospel, and as the awful realities of sin and the cross and judgment and hell are made vivid before them, they are impressed, stirred, moved. But they walk out the door and say it was a good sermon; they only smite their breasts and go away. It takes more than a pious gesture to save the soul. In Luke 18: 13 I read of another man who smote his breast, but he followed it with a prayer, "God, be merciful to me a sinner," and he went home justified. The people smote their breasts and went home terrified; the publican smote his breast and went away justified because he followed it with confession and prayer for mercy. It does no good to be impressed and smite your breast unless you follow it with humility and confession and prayer for pardon.

But there was another at the cross who went still farther. Combining the different accounts of the centurion, we find that he did four things that lead to conversion. He not only was impressed, but he gave expression to his impression, yet I do not believe he was saved. First, "he feared greatly," but "the devils also believe, and tremble" (James 2: 19). Fear may lead to conversion as with the Philippian jailer, but fear not followed by faith is of no avail. Next, the centurion declared, "Certainly this was a righteous man," (Luke 23: 47) but that was only an opinion about Christ, and it is not an opinion about Christ but faith in Christ that saves. Furthermore, he called Christ the Son of God, but since men may call Him Lord and do not what He commands, so this may have been only a wordy tribute of the lips inspired by the moment. He that believes Jesus is the Son of God has life through His name (John 20: 31); God dwells in him (I John 4: 15); he overcomes the world (I John 5: 5) and has the witness in himself (I John 5:10). But there is all the difference in the world between believing with the heart unto righteousness and merely uttering a lofty sentiment under great excitement. Finally, the centurion glorified God, but although God, Who makes even the wrath of men to praise Him, received glory, this may have been glorifying Him with the lips and not with the heart. It is possible to say, "Lord, Lord," and be told, "I never knew you."

Of course, if the centurion believed with his heart, he was saved. But it is possible to make all four of these expressions concerning Christ and not be saved. One may fear, call Christ righteous, call Him the Son of God, and even glorify God under the pressure of the moment, and still be lost.

But we come to one who was saved beyond a doubt, the penitent thief (Luke 23: 39-43). The Scriptures record but one case of "death-bed repentance," "one that none may despair, and only one that none may presume." Here was a criminal, the vilest of the vile. But of all the throng that witnessed the death of our Lord, the lowest character was the only one saved that day. Truly, "not many mighty and noble are called." How simple was his prayer! He only asked to be remembered, not given a place in the kingdom as had been asked for James and John. He did not even ask to be let in—just remembered. Abraham said to Dives, "Son, remember." The only way to avoid having to hear that hereafter is to pray, "Lord, remember," now!

How gracious was our Lord's reply! "Today shalt thou be with me in paradise." There has been much argument as to paradise, where and what it is. Is it not enough that He said, "Thou shalt be *with me*"? Wherever He is will be paradise!

So the first person to enter paradise after Jesus was this thief, not some dignitary of earth, some man of wealth and position. The first recruit for glory was a criminal! Is it not in keeping with the whole tenor of the gospel that this should be the case? The friend of publicans and sinners died first. He had to die first or the thief never would have died, for no one ever died in the presence of Jesus. But on that very day the first to follow Him into the glory was the basest character at Calvary. Verily, God hath chosen the base and despised that no flesh should glory in His presence. No wonder that we sing:

> *Amazing grace, how sweet the sound,*
> *That saved a wretch like me!*

Of all the groups at the cross considered thus far, I would rather have been this thief ten thousand times than any other. Little did the Roman soldiers and haughty Pharisees and indifferent people who passed by dream that the man who got most from that awful day was the very last man anyone would have imagined to be in line for a blessing. It has been thus through the ages. Those who have gotten most from Calvary have been those who came just as they were without one plea but that His blood was shed for them.

> *The dying thief rejoiced to see*
> *That fountain in his day;*
> *And there may I, though vile as he,*
> *Wash all my sins away.*

Finally, all who plunge beneath that fountain filled with blood belong to the last group at Calvary, those who loved Him, His acquaintance, and the women who followed Him from Galilee (Luke 23:49), His mother and John the beloved. I am glad that on that day He was not utterly forsaken; a few who loved Him stood by.

Are you among those who love Him? You sing, "Oh, How I Love Jesus," but do you love Him crucified, and what does His cross mean to you? It is one thing to sing "The Old Rugged Cross" on Sunday morning; it is another to survey that wondrous cross on which the Prince of glory died and count our richest gain but loss and pour contempt on all our pride. It is one thing to talk about His love . . . . and what a love it is! "Herein is love, not that we loved God, but that he loved us, and sent His Son to be the propitiation for our sins" (I John 4: 10).

> *Call back all days of the ages,*
> *All snowflakes come down from above,*
> *All flowers of summer departed,*
> *But think not to measure His love.*

It is easy to talk of such love, but such love demands something from us.

> *Were the whole realm of nature mine,*
> *That were a present far too small;*
> *Love so amazing, so divine,*
> *Demands my soul, my life, my all.*

Who loves Jesus, anyway? "He that hath my commandments and keepeth them, he it is that loveth me" (John 14: 21). "If ye love me, keep my commandments" (John 14: 15). "If a man love me, he will keep my words" (John 14: 23). How do we love

Jesus? The natural man does not, cannot love Jesus, but "unto us who believe, He is precious" (I Pet. 2: 7). We first must receive Him into our hearts as Saviour, then "the love of God is shed abroad in our hearts by the Holy Ghost which is given unto us" (Rom. 5: 5). And we prove that we love Jesus by loving one another (John 13: 35) with a practical love that really helps (I John 4: 19-21).

Where do you stand at Calvary? After all, there are but two classes at the cross: those who rest upon the work our Lord accomplished for salvation and those who reject the provisions of His love. There is a sense in which, while we are *at* the cross, we also are *on* the cross. "His own self bare our sins in his own body on the tree" (I Pet. 2: 24). Why? "That we, being dead to sins, should live unto righteousness." Paul said, "I am crucified with Christ" (Gal. 2: 20) because his self-life was nailed to the tree in the body of Christ.

He just put Himself in your place and mine. His work there is a finished work. Will you believe it and rest upon it and commit yourself to the Great Shepherd and Bishop of your soul? Where are you at Calvary?

XI

"BUT GOD—"

In the second chapter of Ephesians the inspired writer sets before us a marvelous contrast. In the first three verses he describes our wretched state apart from the grace of God. He piles one phrase upon another to picture our lost and undone condition. We were "dead in trespasses and sins"; we walked "according to the course of this world, according to the prince of the power of the air, the spirit that now worketh in the children of disobedience"; we "had our conversation (lit., manner of life) in times past in the lusts of our flesh, fulfilling the desires of the flesh and of the mind"; we "were by nature the children of wrath, even as others."

Can you imagine a more formidable array of words, a more terrible stacking of expressions to declare the state of mortal man apart from redeeming grace? Now if the writer had stopped there, if no more could be said, if we were left shut up in those dismal phrases, then life would be but another name for death and earth but the anteroom to hell.

But verse four opens with two words that spell the difference between life and death, between sin and salvation, between heaven and hell: *"But God—"!* Sin was black, *but God* came in and God is light; Satan was powerful *but God* came in, and God is almighty! Man was lost, *but God* came in and God found him! Man was under wrath, *but God* came in and God is love!

The course of history revolves around these precious words. There was a day when the earth was without form and void, *but God* said, "Let there be light," and there was light. There was a day when "the wickedness of man was great in the earth, and . . . . every imagination of the thoughts of his heart was only evil continually," *but God* chose Noah and gave the race a new start. There was a day when again men forgot God and walked by sight, *but God* called Abraham to set out not knowing whither he went, looking for a city which hath foundations, whose builder and maker is God. There was a day when the chosen people languished under Egyptian bondage, *but God* called Moses to endure as seeing Him who is invisible. There was a day when the backsliding people hung their harps on willows in foreign exile, *but God* raised up Ezekiel and Daniel. There was a day when it seemed that heaven had ceased speaking to earth, *but God* returned on the banks of Jordan to thunder through the voice of John the Baptist.

And then there was the day of all days when man wallowed in sin without a Saviour, groped in darkness without light, struggled in bondage without redemption, *but God* sent forth His Son to live and die and live again, the Just for the unjust, the Sinless for sinners, God for man!

Since that glad day, no matter how low the clouds have hung, no matter how dark the night, nor dreary the age, just when everything has seemed hopeless, history has always turned a corner with those blessed words, *"But God—."* There came a day when the early church seemed to face an impenetrable Gentile world, *but God* struck down a rebel on the Damascus road to make Saul of Tarsus the spearhead of world evangelization. There came a time when the Bible was chained, and superstition took the place of the gospel, *but God* called Wycliffe and Tyndale to loosen His Word in the language of the common people. There came a day when ecclesiasticism threatened to choke the church and when ignorance bound millions in the clutches of the law, *but God* touched a miserable monk, worn out with trying to earn his own salvation, and Martin Luther rose in the strength of the Lord to declare, "The just shall live by faith!" Again, there came a time when the notes of free grace were lost in an age of worldliness and the church had lost the spirit of power in the lap of Delilah, *but God* woke up another groping preacher, and John Wesley warmed his heart at Luther's fire and went out on horseback to carry the gospel to a needy world.

There never has been an age so hopeless but that just when it looked as though the devil had had the last word and hell had turned the tables on heaven, the historian has always been able to turn a new page and write at the top, *"But God—."* And although we live in the midst of world apostasy, the world's Saturday night will turn into God's good-morning, for in that blackest hour just before daylight everything may seem to be lost, *but God* is coming in the Person of His Son to receive from the world His own.

What is true in general has been true in particular in the experience of individual believers. In the darkest hour, those who trust in the Lord have been able to turn from distress to Deity and say, *"But God—."* The Psalmist laments of enemies who speak evil of him, who wonder when he will die and his name perish, who say an evil disease cleaves to him. But from such a sad plight he turns to cry, *"But thou, O Lord—"* (Ps. 41: 4 - 10). Again, he groans in affliction: His days are consumed, his bones burned, he is like a pelican of the wilderness, an owl of the desert, a sparrow alone upon the housetop. Thus he moans over his sad state, but he turns presently to cry, *"But thou, O Lord,* shalt endure forever" (Ps. 102: 1-12). Jeremiah pines in his Lamentation over the pitiful state of the land, in eighteen verses of pure misery (Lam. 5: 1-18) but he turns to rejoice, crying, *"Thou, O Lord,* remainest forever." Micah paints a picture of times so dismal that he reminds us of Elijah under the juniper: The good man is perished; the rulers are in sinful collusion, not even friends, not even wives, may be trusted. Then he turns upward with, "Therefore I will look unto the Lord; I will wait for the God of my salvation: my God will hear me." All else fails . . . *but God!*

As you look back over your life, I am sure that you have occasion to thank God for the unnumbered times when everything else had failed, *but God* came to the rescue. Health had broken — *but God!* Your friends had deceived you — *but God!* Business had failed—*but God!* Loved ones had passed away—*but God!* And right there is the shame of our lives today, that when God has proved Himself again and again a very present help in time of trouble, we should leave Him out of our calculations and measure our undertakings without reckoning on that unseen factor—*But God.* Too often He is a last resort, and prayer is a final expedient, as with the elderly woman who in her illness was told, "You must trust God," and who replied, "Has it come to that?"

We "reason" among ourselves "because we have no bread," and forget Him who spreads a table in the wilderness. We measure the situation by the size of the enemy and forget to say, as did King Asa, "Lord, it is nothing with thee to help, whether with many, or with them that have no power." We decide just about how much we can or cannot do and be, and we limit it all with the old alibis, "Yes, but my family—"; "Yes, but my nerves—"; "Yes, but my circumstances—." Why not put it the other way, "Yes, *but God!*" If God be for us, who can be against us?" What if everybody has failed us so that we must say with Paul, "No man stood with me, but all men forsook me"? Let us move on with him and say, "*Notwithstanding, the Lord* stood with me"! What if men do conspire against us? Let us say to them as did Joseph to his brethren: "Ye thought evil against me; *but God* meant it for good!" So may our experiences begin like the Negro spiritual, "Nobody knows de trouble I see," but end as it ends with, "Glory, glory, hallelujah."

Adoniram Judson caught a vision of evangelizing Burma. "Impossible," you say. Certainly, *if you leave out God.* Moody, starting to England on his first evangelistic mission, said, "I go to win ten thousand souls to Jesus Christ." "Impossible," do you say? Yes, . . . *but God!* Why do we today not follow in the train of these giants of old? We are afraid—afraid to attempt great things for God and expect great things from God. Moses argued with the Almighty in such terms as these: "Yes, but I am not eloquent; yes, but they will not listen to me." God answered, "Say . . ., I AM hath sent me unto you." In other words, it is as if the Lord said, "It is not a matter of who you are but of who I AM." So in our unworthiness, let us, like Amos of old, say, "I was no prophet, neither was I a prophet's son: but I was a herdman, and a gatherer of sycamore fruit: *And the Lord took me.*" Nothing in myself . . . *but God!*

To the sinner, let this picture reveal your lost condition. Read these terrific verses in Eph. 2: 1-3 again. You may seem to be very much alive, but God says you are "dead in trespasses and sins." You may be moral and idealistic, but God says you walk "according to the course of this world." You may recognize the fact of God and His Christ, but God says you walk "according to the prince of the power of the air, the spirit that now worketh in the children of disobedience." You may seem decent and respectable and claim to be a character of integrity, but if you are without Christ, God says your manner of life is in the lusts of the flesh and mind. You may talk of the fatherhood of God and deny the fact of hell and judgment, but God says you are a child of wrath even as others.

But, thank God, the Scripture does not end there. Wretched may be your state and hopeless your condition, *but God* has done something about it. Black indeed was the night of sin, *but God* sent His Son to be the Light of the world. Grievous indeed was our bondage to sin, *but God* sent His Son to be our deliverer. Awful indeed was the guilt of sin, *but God* sent His Son to be our substitute. Sin has abounded, *but God* has seen to it that grace did much more abound. And if in simple faith we turn from sin to this Saviour and receive Him, then the rest of this precious passage becomes our own: *"But God,* who is rich in mercy, for his great love wherewith he loved us, even when we were dead in sins, hath quickened us together with Christ (by grace ye are saved;) and hath raised us up together, and made us sit together in heavenly places in Christ Jesus: that in the ages to come he might show the exceeding riches of his grace, in his kindness toward us, through Christ Jesus" (Eph. 2: 4-7).

No human merit could earn this blessing; no works of the flesh could purchase this treasure, "for by grace are ye saved through faith; and that not of yourselves: it is the gift of God" (vs. 8). How blessed to be able to say, "Once I was blind, *but God* touched me. Once I was lost, *but God* found me. Once I was under wrath, *but God* loved me. Once I was under guilt, *but God* forgave me. Once I was dead, *but God* gave me life. Once I walked according to the course of this world, *but God* turned me and now I walk as He walked. Once I walked according to the prince of the power of the air, *but God* stopped me, and now I follow the Prince of peace. Once I had my manner of life in the lusts of the flesh and mind, *but God* gave me a new life, and Christ liveth in me. Once I was by nature the child of wrath, *but God* has begotten me into the family of love." And all of this is the free gift of grace if one will by faith in God's Son come to that second birthday, the beginning of a new life that opens with those two precious words: *"But God . . ."*

XII

"FAITH IN CHRIST JESUS"

It is a sick and sad and sinful world. There are plenty of specialists doctoring the sickness, but they are treating the symptoms, not the disease. Someone has said that if all the experts were laid in a row, they never would reach a conclusion! This sick old world is being treated with all the panaceas of countless isms and fads and cults and, all the while, the patient sinks lower for the need of a "few things for certain."

In the midst of it all stands the Great Physician of the soul Who is the answer to every need, the solution of every problem. By Him all things consist, in Him dwells all the fulness of the Godhead bodily. In Him are hid all the treasures of wisdom and knowledge. But men will not receive Him, will not come to Him that they might have life, loving darkness rather than light because their deeds are evil.

Since Jesus Christ is the answer to the world's need, and since by faith we receive Him, therefore the world's misery today is due entirely to what is covered in the Scriptural phrase, "because of unbelief."

Four times it occurs in the New Testament with application each time to a different group of humanity, and the four passages cover the whole race. In Rom. 11:20 we read that "because of unbelief" Israel was broken off, set aside nationally in this present age of grace. The Jews rejected their Messiah, the gospel turned to the Gentile world. God is taking out from the Gentiles a people for His Name. So "because of unbelief" Israel is broken off as a nation until the fulness of the Gentiles be come in.

In Matt. 13:58 we read that the Lord Jesus did no mighty works in Nazareth "because of their unbelief." This covers the whole unsaved world. Only one thing hinders the power of Christ — human unbelief. He wants to save and sanctify men and live His life in them, but He cannot do His mighty works because of unbelief. Mark tells us in the same connection that He marveled because of their unbelief. How He must marvel today at an indifferent world that calls Him merely the carpenter's son!

In Heb. 3:19 we read that the Jews who came out of Egypt with Moses could not enter Canaan "because of unbelief." Here the application is to Christians who stand on Jordan's stormy banks but do not follow Christ, our Joshua, into the Canaan of a triumphant Christian experience whereby they reign in life by one, Jesus Christ. The land is ours, but "because of unbelief" Christians fail to trust the promises and take their possessions.

In Matt. 17:20 we read that the disciples could not cast out the evil spirit from the demon-possessed boy because of their unbelief. For the same reason Christians and churches stand powerless before the forces of evil today. What text could better describe our plight than Mark's expression about these same disciples, *"and they could not"*? The pope boasted to Sir Thomas Aquinas, "No longer need the church say, 'Silver and gold have I none,'" but Sir Thomas wisely answered, "True, but neither can she say, 'Rise and walk!'" Just as the Lord Jesus can do no mighty works for us "because of unbelief," neither can we do mighty works for Him for the same reason!

So unbelief accounts for all the world's need. Jews nationally are broken off, the unsaved fail to know the power of Christ, unhappy Christians do not live in the Promised Land, weak Christians cannot prevail against the devil — and all "because of unbelief." Truly we need to pray, "Lord, I believe: help Thou mine unbelief!" *Matt 9:24*

If this be true, then of course the converse is true, that the way out is found in that word of our Lord's: "According to your faith be it unto you" (Matt. 9:29). We go from book to book, from lecture to lecture; we devour devotional volumes, hoping to find on the very next page the magic secret of the life abundant, and all the while here is the key, and there is no other. Your life will be in proportion to your faith.

"According to your faith"— not "according to your fate," as the "bent-twig philosophers" of today would have us believe. Not "according to your fortune," for "a man's life consisteth not in the abundance of the things which he possesseth"; faith goes in where finance cannot tread. It is not "according to your fame," for the only success is in the Spirit, and "he that ruleth his spirit is greater than he that taketh a city." It is not "according to your friends," for popularity and "pull" cannot bring life, and our own familiar friend, in whom we trusted and who did eat of our bread, may lift up his heel against us. Happy are we if, like this Psalmist, we can go on to say, "But thou, O Lord, be merciful unto me and raise me up"!

Nor does our verse read, "According to your feelings." Ah, there is our pet false measure! We substitute wishful thinking for practical trusting and forget that "if wishes were horses, then beggars would ride." Our feelings rise and fall like a thermometer in April, and so does the experience of the Christian who knows how he feels better than he knows Whom he has believed.

After all, it is not a matter of where you are, how you are, who you are, what you are, but *whose* you are. If "ye are Christ's," then "all things are yours."

So it is "according to your faith." But what kind of faith? Faith is a fetish with many people who say it doesn't matter much what you believe just so you believe tremendously in something. But it is not the quality of faith that gives value nor the quantity (for as much as a grain of mustard seed will move mountains) but it is the *object* of faith that matters. One might as well close his eyes and look around on the inside of his head to see sight as to look around inside his heart to see faith. You see something and you know you have sight; you believe something and know you have faith. The real value of faith to the subject depends upon the object.

It is not enough to say, "According to your faith be it unto you," unless you keep this in mind: "All things are possible to him that believeth" only if he believes in Him with Whom all things are possible! The only faith that saves and satisfies is faith in Jesus Christ, for only He is worthy of absolute trust, and only He can meet our need. Nor is it so much faith like Jesus had as faith in Jesus, for while He is an example of faith, He is more; He is the object of faith. So, while "we walk by faith and not by sight," and while "the just shall live by faith," the emphasis is on the Object, and the entire Christian experience may be summed up in the words "faith in Christ Jesus" (Gal. 3:26).

It begins with faith in Christ Jesus as Saviour. "Believe on the Lord Jesus Christ, and thou shalt be saved" (Acts 16:31). "Repentance toward God" must be accompanied by "faith toward our Lord Jesus Christ" (Acts 20:21). "Faith cometh by hearing, and hearing by the Word of God" (Rom. 10:17). The sinner, hearing the Word, is convicted and brought to repentance. But hearing the Word is not enough: it must be mixed with faith (Heb. 4:2). Faith looks unto the Lord Jesus, receives Him into the heart, commits all to Him. "By grace are ye saved through faith," and even that faith is "not of yourselves: it is the gift of God" (Eph. 2:8).

Of course this involves mysteries, but believing faith is simple on our part — unless we try to understand it! Simple souls just trust Jesus, while philosophers try to unravel it and never trust. When the sinner, convicted and in godly sorrow and repentance, quits trying and begins trusting, he finds " 'tis done, the great transaction's done."

But why must we believe in Jesus Christ? Why is there no salvation in any other? Why is there "none other name under heaven given among men whereby we must be saved"? Because of Who God is, to begin with. God is love, but He is also just and holy, and He has a standard of righteousness that must be met if men are to be saved. God could not be just and holy if He allowed men to be saved according to a lower standard than His own. Man through sin has broken God's law, has become corrupt and fallen far below God's mark: "All have sinned and come short of the glory of God." If man is to be saved, someone who is sinless and can meet God's standard of righteousness on one hand and yet one who can identify himself with sinful man and become sin though not sinful on the other hand must pay the penalty of sin. That is exactly why Jesus is our Saviour, because of Who He is and what He did. He was Son of God and Son of man, and He shed His blood a ransom for many and bare our sins in His own body on the tree. Yet it was the good Father Who gave His only-begotten Son, and so wonderful is His grace that the moment we receive Christ God accepts us and counts us as though we had never sinned. But we never could be saved by faith in anyone else, for only Jesus was Son of God and Son of man, and Jesus alone could truly die for the sins of the world.

All the blessings of salvation come through simple faith in Jesus Christ. Regeneration is through Him, for we are "children of God by faith in Christ Jesus" (Gal. 3:26) and "as many as received him, to them gave he power to become the sons of God, even to them that believe on his name" (John 1:12). Justification is through Him by faith, for God is the justifier of them which believe in Jesus (Rom. 3:26) "and by *him* all that *believe* are justified from all things" (Acts 13:39). We are "not justified by the works of the law but by the faith of Jesus Christ" (Gal. 2:16). Righteousness is through Him by faith, for Christ is made unto us righteousness (I Cor. 1:30). We have no righteousness of our own that God will accept, but when we believe Christ's righteousness becomes our own and we have "righteousness which is of God by the *faith of Jesus Christ*" (Rom. 3: 22; Phil. 3: 9). Eternal life is through Him by faith, for "whosoever believeth in him should not perish but have everlasting life" (John 3:16) and "he that *believeth* on *him* has eternal life" (John 6:47).

So all this cluster of blessings hangs upon simple faith in Jesus Christ. But one does not have to wait until he understands all this to receive the fruit of it. The natural man cannot receive these things anyway— one may as well try to describe a sunset to a blind man — so the supreme thing is not to understand it but to stand on it. The devil always seeks to get a man seeking salvation off on a by-path of questioning along such a line as: If faith comes from God, how can I believe? God gives air and lungs to breathe it but He doesn't breathe for us: He gives eternal life and faith to take it, but He doesn't do our believing for us.

After all, we are saved not by a plan of salvation but by a Person, and we are sadly beside the point when we try to understand the plan and process instead of coming to the Person and receiving the possession. When I was saved, a small boy in the Carolina woods, I did not understand much about the mysteries of redemption, and I don't yet, but I came to Jesus as I was, weary and worn and sad; I found Him a resting-place and He made me glad. He Himself gave us both sides of this great matter when He said, "All that the Father giveth me shall come to me." There is the sublimity of God's side of it, "and him that cometh to me I will in no wise cast out. There is the simplicity of our side of it!

Faith in Christ Jesus not only receives Him as Saviour but as Keeper. Not only are we saved through faith, but we are "kept by the power of God through faith unto salvation" (I Pet. 1:5). Paul was persuaded that He Whom he had believed was able to keep. What does He keep? That which we commit unto Him. As much as we commit, He keeps. He not only keeps our souls in eternal security, but He keeps us amid the problems that beset us daily in proportion as faith commits them unto Him and looks unto Him to keep.

Four times did our Lord use the phrase, "O ye of little faith" in the Gospels, and each time it applies to some common problem of every-day experience. In Matt. 6: 30, He said, "Wherefore, if God so clothe the grass of the field, which today is, and tomorrow is cast into the oven, shall he not much more clothe you, O ye of little faith?" Here faith in Him is the answer to care. He said, "Let not your heart be troubled: ye believe in God, *believe* also in *me*." We pretend that we cannot help being troubled, but He would not have said, *"Let not* your heart be troubled," if we could not help it. We are to cast all our care upon God, for He careth for us. Caring for us is God's business, so why not let Him do it!

To the alarmed disciples on the stormy sea (Matt. 8: 26) He said, "Why are ye fearful, O ye of little faith?" Here faith is the answer to fear. I have heard this incident used to illustrate the need of calling Christ, dormant in the life, into action. But if these disciples had had stronger faith, they would not have awakened the Lord; they would have let Him sleep, confident that with Him present no harm could befall them.

When we are fearful, we are not believing. "There is no fear in love; but perfect love casteth out fear: because fear hath torment. He that feareth is not made perfect in love" (I John 4: 18). Now, faith worketh by love, according to Gal. 5: 6; so faith, working by love, casts out fear. We would expect this verse to say he that feareth is not made perfect in courage or in faith, but it says "love." Love is the way faith works—faith's expression.

In Matt. 14:31, our Lord said to Peter, as He rescued him from sinking, "O thou of little faith, wherefore didst thou doubt?" Here faith is the opposite of doubt. Faith walks the waves toward Jesus. Doubt stays in the boat, dabbling first this foot, then that, in the water, afraid of sinking. But suppose you even should take a fainting spell and sink, you won't drown!

Of course Peter got his eyes off the Lord. We are to "consider Him" lest we "faint in our minds." The devil took the form of a serpent and raised first a doubt: "Yea, hath God said?" Jesus took the form of a servant and took His stand on what God hath said. We doubt because we see circumstance: "The well is deep .... he hath been dead four days .... this is the third day since these things were done . . ." —consider how circumstances loomed greater than the Lord! But He ever stands by the grave of the impossible, saying, "Said I not unto thee, that, if thou wouldest *believe, thou* shouldest *see* the glory of God?"

In Matt. 16:8 Jesus said to His disciples: "O ye of little faith, why reason ye among yourselves, because ye have brought no bread?" They had just seen Him feed the multitudes, yet now they were worried because they had no bread. Is that not a perfect picture of Christians today, singly or as churches, panicky over lack of this and that! There is "nothing to set before" our friends who have come in their journey, ... and yet there is plenty and to spare in the Father's house. He spreads tables in the wilderness. He replenishes the meal in the barrel! We reason among ourselves; we hold conferences and appoint committees; we worry about how to get people to church, how to reach the young, how to pay our bills; we confer and discuss our lack of bread as though we had no Christ Who fed thousands with almost nothing and by Whom our God has promised to supply all our needs!

Truly He must say, "O ye of little faith, worried, fearful, doubting, panicky . . . . how is it that ye do not believe?" Must not God be saying of us as to Israel, "How long will it be ere they believe me?" (Num. 14: 11).

No matter which way you look, the answer to any and every need and problem and question is by *faith* in *Christ Jesus*. How shall we overcome the world? "Who is he that overcometh the world, but he that *believeth* that *Jesus* is the Son of God?" (I John 5:5). How shall we live the victorious life? "They which *receive* abundance of grace and the gift of righteousness shall reign in life by one, Jesus Christ" (Rom. 5: 17). Do you need holiness? It is "By *faith* that is in *me*," he declared (Acts 26:18), even the fulness of the Spirit they which *believe* on *Him* shall receive (John 7: 39).

He Himself declared again and again that it is our faith that appropriates from Him the blessing. To the woman anointing Him, He said, "Thy faith hath saved thee" (Luke 7: 50): faith brings forgiveness. To the leper, He said, "Thy faith hath made thee whole" (Luke 17: 19). He said it also to the woman healed of the issue of blood (Matt. 9: 22) and to Bartimaeus (Mark 10: 52): faith brings healing. To the Syrophenician woman, He declared: "O woman, great is thy faith: be it unto thee even as thou wilt" (Matt. 15:28). Faith brings blessing to others as it did here to her daughter.

What we ask in prayer, believing, we shall receive (Matt. 21:22). We must ask in faith unwavering (James 1:6). It is significant that when the disciples asked the Lord to increase their faith, He answered, "If ye *had* faith as a grain of mustard seed, ye might say unto this sycamore tree, Be thou plucked up by the root, and be thou planted in the sea; and it should obey you" (Luke 17:6). He demands that we exercise the faith we have, stretch forth our hand, rise, take up the bed and walk, put our belief into action, be not faithless but believing.

We sing about faith in Jesus, pray about it, pay preachers to preach about it, but we live much as the world does, by our own wits and resources, and the life of faith is only a pious phrase, lovely but impractical. All the while the Lord stands among us marveling at our unbelief, asking, "Believe ye that I am able to do this?" saying, "Be not afraid, only believe," "If thou canst believe, all things are possible to him that believeth."

The whole Christian experience is simply Christ Himself in the believer. "To me to live is Christ," said Paul, and this life he lived by the faith of the Son of God. The work of God is that we *believe* on *Him* Whom God hath sent (John 6:29). It is simply that we look unto Him first for salvation and then we cease to live; we have no life of our own; we just look to Him to live His own life in us. Don't you see how that simplifies the whole matter? The responsibility henceforth is His; our health, food, clothes, our wisdom, method, message, results, funds, all these are His concern. He is made unto us wisdom, righteousness, sanctification, redemption. Our joy and peace are simply in believing Him (Rom. 15: 13). It is not that we strive to imitate Him; we simply abide in Him; we travel the T and O Trail — Trust and Obey — and the Holy Spirit works in us the nature of the Lord Jesus. We decrease and He increases as we put on the Lord Jesus and let His mind be in us.

Everything we need is found in Him. Whether you need gentleness, He is meek and lowly, or whether you need boldness and bravery, He is fearless. Whether you are called to the lowly task, just going about doing good, so was He and so did He. But if you are to be a solitary seer, lonely and misunderstood, so was He! By Him all things consist, and we are complete in Him.

It is true that we cannot see Him, *yet believing*, we rejoice with joy unspeakable and full of glory. Faith walks without seeing, but the faith that walks will see. Faith believes what God's Word says about Jesus, acts accordingly, steps out, sink or swim, live or die, feeling, maybe, very weak and doubtless trembling, but steps out just the same while every circumstance makes it look downright foolish and while friends and neighbors caution us lest we become righteous overmuch! But consider Abraham, the father of the faithful and our type through the ages: He went out not knowing whither; against hope he believed in hope; he considered not his own body; he staggered not at the promise of God through unbelief, but was strong in faith, giving glory to God; and being fully persuaded that what He had promised, He was able also to perform — that is faith!

It is evident that we must live some way or other. All other ways are unsatisfactory; they end in despair and destruction. Blessed is the man who comes to holy desperation and cries, "I am undone; I am at the end of my resources. Henceforth, with no 'if's' and 'buts' about it, I stake all on Jesus Christ. I give myself to live by the faith of the Son of God. I now trust Him as my Saviour. I yield to Him as Lord all I am and have that He may sanctify it to His use and glory. Looking unto Jesus for every need, I would know Him and make Him known. I would simply trust and obey, believe in the Lord Jesus Christ and keep His commandments. I will spend and be spent for Him that my life might be a witness to 'faith in Christ Jesus,' 'faith which worketh by love,' love for the Lord, for the brethren, for the lost. My message will be 'Jesus only.' To me to live henceforth is not simply to live like Christ or for Him — to live *is* Christ."

A housewife took a check to the bank and, being asked to endorse it, wrote on the back, "I heartily endorse this check!" Of course, the cashier returned it and said, "You must sign your name." Many today endorse anything the Bible says, accept it intellectually, but have never committed themselves to it! You must sign your own name on the dotted line! "According to *your* faith, be it unto you."

It is a strange world and a puzzling existence, but here is the key: "Faith in Christ Jesus." How long will it be ere you believe Him?

Printed in the United States of America

CPSIA information can be obtained at www.ICGtesting.com
Printed in the USA
LVOW12s1944060814

397852LV00030B/1809/P